The

SAINT JOHN PRAYERBOOK

The SAINT JOHN PRAYERBOOK

Biblical Meditations and Prayers Inspired by the Beloved Disciple

By Fr. Gabriel Mary Fiore, CSJ

TAN Books
Gastonia, North Carolina

Nihil Obstat: Fr. Gonzague de Longcamp, STD

Imprimi Potest: Fr. Francois-Xavier Cazali,
Prior General, Congregation of Saint John,
December 5, 2025

Cover design by Jordan Avery

ISBN: 978-1-5051-3651-7
ePUB ISBN: 978-1-5051-4025-5

Published in the United States by
TAN Books
PO Box 269
Gastonia, NC 28053
www.TANBooks.com

Printed in India

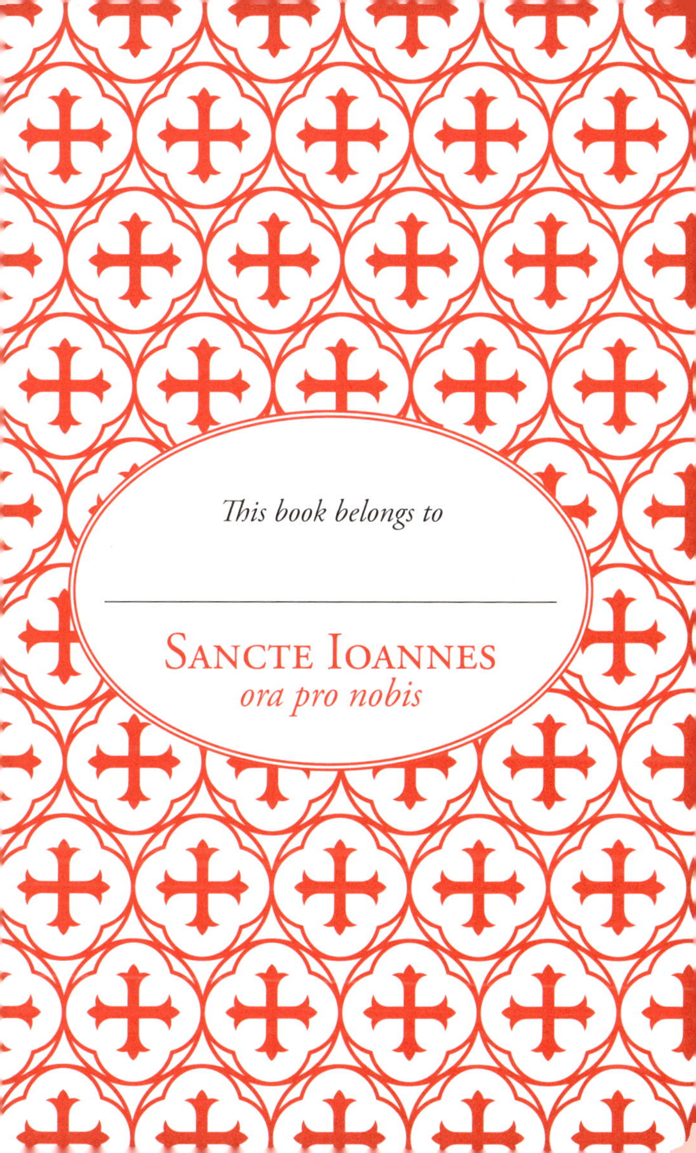
This book belongs to
Sancte Ioannes
ora pro nobis

Permissions

The hymn in the section "Praise for Saint John's Purity of Heart" consists of stanzas four and five from "Hymn to Virginity XV" in Ephrem the Syrian, *Hymns*, trans. Kathleen McVey, Classics of Western Spirituality Series (Paulist Press, 1989), 326–77. Select phrases were altered for clarity and devotional use (see endnote 67). Used with permission.

The prayer of St. Anselm of Canterbury in the section "Prayer to John in Times of Penance" is adapted from "Prayer to St. John the Evangelist (1)", published in *The Prayers and Meditations of St. Anselm with the Proslogion*, trans. Sister Benedicta Ward, SLG (Penguin Classics, 1973), 157–62. Only verses 1–24 and 103–11 were used for brevity and select phrases were retranslated for devotional use (see endnote 72). Used with permission.

The hymn in section "Praise to Share in John's Holiness" is excerpted from the hymn "Gratulemur Ad Festivum", published in *On Love: A Selection of Works of Hugh, Adam, Achard, Richard, and Godfrey of St. Victor*, ed. Hugh Feiss (Brepols Publishers, 2011), 237–39. Only verses 1–5, 14, 15–18 were used for brevity and select words were modified for clarity (see endnote 73). Used with permission.

The prayer in the section "Asking for John's Wisdom and Protection" is excerpt of Prayer of a Benedictine Nun. Jeffrey F. Hamburger, *St. John the Divine: The Deified Evangelist in Medieval Art and Theology* (University of California Press, 2002), 167–69. Only lines 1–10, 12–15, 18–26, 35–59 were used for brevity and two select phrases were modified for clarity (see endnote 76). Used with permission.

The hymn in the section "An Ambrosian Hymn to John the Baptist" is an excerpt from the hymn "Amore Christi

Nobilis". Prosper Guéranger, *The Liturgical Year: Christmas, Book 1*, trans. Laurence Shepherd (Loreto, 2000), 265–66. Only strophes 1-6 were used for brevity and select phrases and words were altered for clarity (see endnote 68). Used with permission.

Bible Translations Used in This Work

CONTENTS

"And let them remember that prayer should accompany the reading of Sacred Scripture, so that God and man may talk together . . ."

—Vatican II, Dei Verbum §25

INTRODUCTION

For centuries, theologians and preachers, poets and mystics have been drawn to St. John the Evangelist. His sacred writings and persona have inspired art and music, sermons and commentary. Still today, the evangelist remains an inspiring source of Christian spirituality. Yet strangely, while many confess admiration or devotion to John, rarely do we turn to him *in prayer.*

Perhaps, John feels too distant and otherworldly to serve as an intercessor or a guide for prayer. Or perhaps his liturgical feast, celebrated on December 27, has become forgotten due to Christmas vacation and travel. Finally, some may have heard a friend or scholar raise questions about the historical identity of Jesus's "beloved disciple," the gospel's presumed evangelist. Yet, for centuries and to this day, the Church honors the evangelist as "John" in her liturgy and canon of Scripture.

John's Writings as a Resource for Prayer

The Church turns to John not only as an intercessor but also as a guide, citing John's writings over one hundred times in her catechesis on prayer.[1] John's writings contain instructions on prayer and worship found nowhere else in the New Testament. Several scholars now believe that the Prologue to John's Gospel was actually a hymn, a primitive Christian prayer; it continues to inspire composers of sacred music. And who can forget Jesus's long, solemn prayer to the Father in John 17, still proclaimed in the liturgy during the days leading up to Pentecost? From John alone do we learn how Christ is adored and worshipped in heaven. And the words of John close the entire canon of sacred Scripture with one last passionate prayer of hope, "Amen! Come Lord Jesus!" (Rev 22:20).

Praying with the Gospel and with the Church

Of the hundreds of contemporary commentaries and meditations on the writings attributed to John, this book offers a unique perspective, inviting readers to *pray with* John's Gospel and helping those who wish to *pray to* John as intercessor. It is my hope that it will serve to rediscover John's Gospel not only as a summit of sacred *theology* but also as an inspiring book for Christian *prayer*.

From the early patristic era to the postmodern world, from the Latin West to the shining East, from Catholics and Orthodox to Reformed Christians, the faithful of Christ have prayed with and to John, both thanking God for His gifts and believing that we too may share in his charism of contemplation and intimacy with Christ.

The prayers found in this book—some composed by myself, others gathered from the ecclesial tradition—all have but one goal: to help readers pray with the inspired words of John's Gospel and to pray with the Church who honors the disciple whom Jesus loved. By praying with John, we can hope to become the worshipers whom the Father seeks (Jn 4:23), to find rest upon Jesus's bosom (13:23) and welcome His invitation to friendship (15:15), to stand by Jesus crucified and respond to His thirst (19:25–29), and to kneel before Christ radiant with heavenly glory (Rev 1:12–18).

Identity Questions and Traditional Piety

I have carefully studied the objections raised against the traditional identification of the fourth evangelist with the apostle John of Zebedee.[2] Having examined alternative proposals for the beloved disciple and the merits of various theories of authorship, I can confidently say that serious scholarship does not undermine traditional piety. Some respected scholars still defend the traditional profile of St. John as the most likely conclusion from the available data. Others, even conservative churchmen like Joseph Ratzinger (Pope Benedict XVI), propose alternative scenarios of shared authorship (e.g., the apostle John had a secretary, etc.) that pose no significant problems for traditional devotion. Non-specialists should not confuse scholarly opinions with established scientific fact. Even after 150 years of critical scholarship, no alternative theory has gained consensus, nor is the historical or literary data said to have "disproved" the traditional view. Thus, believers are left free to judge the matter for themselves based on Scripture and Tradition and can embrace traditional piety without hesitation.

The devotional prayers gathered here merit the respect of theologians and exegetes for the faith that animates them and for the longstanding tradition which they express; a faith that rests not upon this or that name of the evangelist but rather on the reliability of his eyewitness account, on his intimacy with Jesus and perceptive faith, on his faithful discipleship, and on the divine will that his charism and testimony should remain alive in the Church until the day when Jesus comes in glory.

Praying with John to Share in His Charism

For nearly two millennia, devout men and women, mystics (Hildegard, Eriugena), poets (Notker, Adam of St. Victor), and doctors of the Church (Ambrose, Ephrem, Peter Damian, Anselm) have prayed to St. John. Through his example and canonical writings, the Holy Spirit has inspired virtues in believers and an intimacy with Christ like John's. For myself, becoming a brother of St. John has helped me to grow in friendship with Christ. Johannine devotion is not meant to fixate upon the figure of John nor to isolate one part of the sacred canon but rather should lead us closer to Christ whom John loved so dearly.

May the following prayers, inspired by the holy Gospel and gathered from the Christian East and West, incite the faithful to better know John in prayer and to rely on the intercession of him who remains our "brother and companion in the suffering and kingdom and patient endurance that are ours in Jesus" (Rev 1:9 NIV).

How to Use This Book

PART ONE invites readers to *pray with* John. It proposes thirty original prayers composed by the author (me) based on verses from John's Gospel. I selected verses that lend themselves to prayer, because they are petitions addressed to Jesus, confessions of faith, the prayers of Jesus Himself, etc. These prayers are intended to help readers pray with the inspired words of Scripture by making them their own. Each biblical prayer (on the right page) is preceded by a brief prose explanation (on the left page) which situates the selected verse in its original context and prepares the reader to pray with it.

The approach adopted here is the centuries old practice of *lectio divina*, whereby a short passage from sacred Scripture is read in a slow, prayerful way through successive stages of *lectio* (listening to what the verse or passage means based in its context); *meditatio* (prayerfully considering what this verse says to us personally and as a community); and *oratio* (expressing our own prayerful response to the Word of God); the exercise should culminate in contemplation and action.

Readers may wish to use one these meditations per day over a course of thirty days, making something of an extended retreat with John's Gospel.

PART TWO is a resource for those readers who wish to *pray to* John as heavenly intercessor. It presents thirty hymns and devotional prayers addressed to God or directly to St. John the Evangelist by various Christian writers from the early patristic era to the present day. Most translations are my own from original language sources. I have often taken the liberty of abbreviating or making minor amendments to the original prayers to render them more fluid and suitable for devotional use. To avoid distracting devotional readers with brackets and footnotes, references to the source material and details of my amendments are found at the back of the book. For prayers composed in English, I have opted to leave archaic formulations (thy, thee, etc.).

It is quite possible that other hymns and prayers to St. John exist that I did not encounter when assembling this collection. Readers are encouraged to send those references to the author, so that they might be incorporated into a later edition of this book.

It is my hope that this collection will nourish the piety of individuals and communities who hold St. John dear and who continue to be inspired by his sacred writings and example of loving discipleship.

Fr. Gabriel Mary Fiore, CSJ
December 27, 2025,
feast of St. John the Evangelist

PART ONE

Praying with St. John's Gospel

"Prayer . . . is the primary way by which the word transforms us."
—Pope Benedict XVI, Verbum Domini §87

JOHN'S PROLOGUE AS PRAYER

From the time of the early Church Fathers, the prologue of John's Gospel (1:1–18) has inspired admiration. These majestic verses transport the prayerful reader beyond the created world, space and time, and far from our temporal concerns into the eternal mystery of God Himself.

Thanks to John's inspired contemplation, it is as if the veil of faith is pulled aside for a moment, giving us a glimpse of Jesus's eternal generation as God's Only Son. The prologue also gives us a divine outlook on the created world, Jesus's saving mission, and our response of faith.

As revelation about God, Christ, and ourselves, this sacred text is also food for meditation and prayer. John's solemn prologue is considered by many scholars to be an *ancient Christian hymn.*[3] It is "a piece of cultic-liturgical poetry, oscillating between the language of revelation and confession."[4] In this prologue, we listen to the early Christian community "sing" its response to the coming of Jesus; we are also invited to identify with John who "bears witness" and "cries out" to the world the mystery of Christ's divinity.[5] As we pray this solemn hymn, we are united to believers across the centuries who have used these words to profess our common faith: "From his fullness we have all received grace upon grace . . ." (Jn 1:16).

Here, I have selected only a few verses from John's prologue to inspire prayer. Readers may continue the exercise, allowing the Spirit to bring to life other verses as prayers of adoration and praise.

"And we have seen his glory . . ." (Jn 1:14)[6]

Here, the evangelist is likely speaking on behalf of Jesus's early disciples. Living alongside Him for three years, they caught glimmers of His divine glory through impressive signs and miracles. At Cana, Jesus "revealed his glory" (Jn 2:11). Before raising Lazarus, He promised that the grieving sisters would "see the glory of God" (Jn 11:40). His closest disciples were dazzled by His splendor on Mount Tabor, and all of them saw Him rise into heaven. Later, on Patmos, John again saw His face blazing like the sun (Rev 1:16) . . . "And we have seen his glory!"

And yet, John insists that no one has ever seen God (Jn 1:18). To understand this paradox, it helps to recall that John learned to "see glory" in realities that would not appear glorious to the human eye: he heard the Father (Jn 12:29) and Jesus (Jn 13:31; 17:1) speak of the Son's darkest moments as a "glorification"; he learned by grace to perceive Jesus's divinity hidden in His humble humanity; he recognized new life springing from the Lord's pierced side (Jn 19:34) and victory resounding from His empty tomb (Jn 20:9).

So, we too have seen His glory. As our spiritual eyes are healed from sin and adjust to the light of faith, we too have seen. As we look and listen to Jesus, as we adore and confess Him, more and more we begin to "see" Him in faith.

O beloved disciple of Jesus, share with us your contemplative heart, your faith that sees!

HOLY FATHER, in the many times when, after the betrayal of sin, Your Son has washed our feet and souls clean, we have seen His glory!

When He has called forth a lost brother from the dark depths of despair or raised a crippled soul who had no one to help, we have seen His glory!

Every time He has changed the "waters" of service into the "good wine" of joy; when we are battling the stormy seas, and He calms the waters; when negligent and defiant we have pierced Him through, but clement and triumphant He unleashes Your rivers of mercy; when we have faced an empty tomb, but He awakens us by calling our name; time and again, we have seen His glory!

May our sight never fail, may our pride never blind us. Open our eyes, so that we may trust and recognize You at work in hidden ways, until that day when we at last shall be like unto Him, for we will have seen His glory! +

"And from his fullness we have all received, grace upon grace" (Jn 1:16)[7]

As God's only begotten Son, Jesus is "full of grace" (Jn 1:14). His holy humanity is united to God (Jn 10:30) and possesses the fullness of the Spirit (Jn 3:34). "Grace" also refers to God's free choice to save us and to shower upon us in Christ "every spiritual blessing" (Eph 1:3–8). Jesus has come to give believers not only a share in His own "life to the full" (Jn 10:10) but also the Spirit's ongoing assistance. Grace upon grace!

John's phrase suggests one divine favor after another, an inexhaustible supply of blessings and saving graces. Time and again, God saved His people from peril, forgave them, and restored them to His friendship. He has done the same for each of us. Grace upon grace!

St. John Chrysostom enlightens "grace upon grace" with the Gospel's image of living water:

> *He is Himself the very fountain . . . not retaining within Himself the riches of His good things but overflowing with them into all the others. And even after the overflowing, He still remains full . . . streaming forth as much as ever and imparting to others a share of these blessings.*[8]

At the cross, John contemplated water, blood, and the Spirit flowing from the heart of Jesus (Jn 19:34; 1 Jn 5:6–8), a river of life-giving water nourishing all thirsty souls who come to Christ (Rev 22:1–2,17).

And now that same Spirit—His life, the love and joy He receives from the Father—flows within us believers (Jn 7:39) and freely, without cost. Grace upon grace!

LIKE THE SAMARITAN, I have found the living water for which my soul thirsts. Like the blind man, I have been given to see and to know You. Like Peter, I have failed, but You have beckoned and allowed me to profess my love anew. Like the beloved disciple, You have drawn me, though unworthy, to rest on Your bosom.

God of mercies, time and again, from Your fullness, I have received grace upon grace. Grant me today, to remain in that grace: to drink of You abundantly, to see You in all things, to abide in Your friendship, to find rest in You alone.

Today I give thanks for the mercies You have showered upon those around me. It's a joy to see those searching find You at last, those hardened in their ways reborn in the Spirit, those in darkness called forth from the grave, and those alone served and befriended.

Father, I thank You. By the gift of Your Son and from His fullness, we have all received grace upon grace! +

"The light shines in the darkness, and the darkness did not overcome it" (Jn 1:5)[9]

In the Gospels, "light" symbolizes faith and moral truth, as opposed to the "darkness" of unbelief and sin. Jesus came as a "light" for the nations (Mt 4:16; Lk 2:32), and believers are "sons of light" (Lk 16:8) who must protect the inner "lamp" of their hearts from the "darkness" of selfish attitudes (Mt 6:22–23).

John's Gospel in particular reveals Jesus as the "true light" come to enlighten each person (Jn 1:9). In heaven, His face "shines like the sun" (Rev 1:16), and the Lamb of God is the lamp of the saints (Rev 21:23). Meanwhile, in this earthly life we must learn to "believe" and to "walk" in faith, to become "children of the light" (Jn 12:35–36). Nicodemus, the adulterous woman, and the blind man show it is possible to move from darkness into the light of faith and integrity. Following Jesus brings us "the light of life" (Jn 8:12).

"The light shines in the darkness . . ." is a profession of faith, a celebration of such victories of light in and around us. It reveals a conflict, a high-stakes tug-of-war between forces of truth and sin in our world and in our souls.

As we pray this verse with John and the saints, we adhere firmly to the light of Christ and confess that the victory obtained on the cross will, in the end, win over our hearts and our world: "The light shines in the darkness," and darkness cannot and will not overcome it!

I PRAISE YOU, Lord and Light of the world, for You never cease to shine Your rays of truth and purity among us. By Your grace, the darkness has not overcome.

Yet there is a battle deep within, a menacing pull of selfishness, lust, and pride that, time and again, threatens to extinguish the light You place there. Still, even now, the darkness has not overcome it.

Today, with all my strength of soul, I adhere to the truths of faith and the way of holiness revealed in the Gospel; they are a lamp for my steps.

When I go astray, illumine the right path before me. When I yield to unholy allures, let Your beauty draw more sweetly, and Your truth win the day. Do not allow the ugly, base, and twisted ways of the world to overcome the goodness You have created in and around me. I am willing to fight, but without You I can do nothing.

So let Your light shine in the darkness and the darkness never overcome it! +

PETITIONS ADDRESSED TO JESUS

In John's Gospel, human needs often become the occasion for a life-changing encounter with Christ. Persons in distress turn to Jesus for help, like the royal official whose child is gravely ill (Jn 4:47). At times, Jesus takes the initiative to seek out someone in need, like the paralyzed man (Jn 5:6). It inspires hope to know that the most distressing times in our lives attract Jesus and can become moments of grace.

However, for trying moments to become salvific, suffering itself is not sufficient. We must learn to surrender our needs to Christ with faith and trust, transforming feelings of pain and anxiety into prayers addressed to God.

At the Last Supper, as recorded by John, Jesus insists *six times* that disciples make petitions to God. For example, "Until now you have not asked for anything in my name. Ask and you will receive, so that your joy may be complete" (Jn 16:24). If Jesus insists, it's because petitionary prayer is salvific for us, a place where we discover just how much God is our Father.

In John's Gospel, Jesus meets people in their places of need and desire (for health, water, bread, etc.) and raises them up from those basic concerns to heavenly gifts: from the request for wine to love and joy; from water to the inner life of the Spirit; from earthly bread to the gift of the Eucharist; from mourning to new life.

The following prayers are based on petitions addressed to Jesus by individuals in the Gospel. At the time, they did not all know of Jesus's divinity. Still, we can make those requests our own and, enriched with Christian faith, use them as prayers of petition for ourselves and for others: "Ask and you will receive, so that your joy may be complete."

"They have no wine" (Jn 2:3)

The first petition in John's Gospel is an act of intercession. The Mother of Jesus, recognizing something missing from the festivities, presents that lack to Jesus. To empathize with the needs of others and seek to remedy their distress are acts of charity and spiritual motherhood. St. John Paul II explains:

> *The Cana event outlines what is actually manifested as a new kind of motherhood according to the spirit . . ., that is to say Mary's solicitude for human beings, her coming to them in the wide variety of their wants and needs . . . . This coming to the aid of human need means, at the same time, bringing those needs within the radius of Christ's messianic mission and salvific power.*[10]

Intercessory prayer expands the heart. Others' needs and growth become our concern, and by lifting them up in prayer we are united to Jesus who intercedes for all the faithful (cf. Jn 17:20; 1 Jn 2:1; Heb 7:25).

In the Bible, wine is celebrated for its power to gladden the heart (Ps 104:15). It can symbolize the joys of love (Sg 1:2, 4:10), the blood of the new covenant (Mt 26:28; 1 Cor 11:25), and the future messianic banquet (Is 25:6; Mt 26:29).

We can use this petition to pray for the "good wine" of Christian love and joy wherever it is lacking. When prayer has gone dry, when a faith-community has lost vitality; when a marriage or family is missing love and warmth: "I/We/They have no wine."

LORD JESUS CHRIST, our High Priest, You poured out Your blood as the wine of the new covenant to obtain our salvation and the joys of new life. And yet, many still do not know that life in its fullness. They have no wine.

Have mercy on us sinners. So often we seek pleasure from shallow things that bring no rest to the soul. We wander, because we have not acquired a taste for Your presence in prayer. We have no wine.

Have mercy on our families. We don't know how to give and receive love, to communicate openly, to correct constructively, to forgive unbegrudgingly. So, we avoid home life rather than investing in it. We have no wine.

Have mercy on our churches. You invite us to love one another as You have loved us. And yet we seek power and distrust authority; we demand to be served rather than serving. We struggle to live out the Gospel and fail to attract others to its message.

Lord, come to our aid. We have no wine. +

"Lord, give me this water" (Jn 4:15)[11]

During His dialogue with the Samaritan woman, Jesus pivots from the well-water she has drawn to a promise of "living water" He alone can provide (Jn 4:10). This inner spring would quench every thirst and spring up to eternal life (Jn 4:14). Her desire awakened, the woman dares to ask, "Sir, give me this water!"

John explains that the "living water" promised by Jesus refers to the gift of the Holy Spirit (Jn 7:38–39), and later Christian writers have seen additional spiritual gifts symbolized in this water.

For Origen of Alexandria, Jacob's "well" symbolizes sacred Scripture.[12] By daily biblical mediation, the faithful learn to draw water from this well. This practice may not immediately satisfy our thirst, but we should beg Christ to teach us Himself, to bestow the "living waters" of His Spirit, and to grant us understanding of things divine: "Lord, give me this water!"

St. Teresa of Avila carried with her a pious image of Jesus at the well inscribed with the words: *Domine, da mihi acquam* (Lord, give me water).[13] For Teresa, the "living waters" represent the intimacy with God that results from regular prayer. She exhorts us to persevere in prayer with unshakeable trust in Jesus's promise. Despite her mystical favors, she too knew spiritual thirst: "Do not deny me this sweetest water that You promise to those who want it. I want it, Lord, and I beg for it, and I come to You."

May this petition open for us the floodgates of heaven.

YOURS, LORD, are the flood waters that cleansed creation. Yours are the new waters of baptism. And Yours are the waters of grace poured out at the cross.

You are the fountain that never runs dry. In You is the source of life itself. From Your sacred heart flows every spiritual blessing in the heavens. To this day, You give the Spirit without measure!

For many years now, I have come to Your holy altar for adoration and communion. I have tried to "remain" with You in silent prayer. I listen to Your words in Scripture and join the liturgy of the Church.

Yet a deep, nagging thirst in the pit of my soul still longs to know and to love You, to enjoy You and to rest in You, to hear and to see You. Strangely, that thirst is not quenched by Your many gifts.

And so, dear Lord, give me this water; the living water I need to get through this day; the fountain I can draw upon to serve others. Domine, da mihi acquam! +

"Lord, come down before my child dies" (Jn 4:49)[14]

During His public ministry, Jesus showed a special tenderness for children. So tangible was His goodness that parents would bring their little ones to Jesus for blessings (Mt 19:13–15). When His disciples found this a nuisance, Jesus reproached them, "Let the little children come to me . . ." (Mk 10:13–14).

Christ praises God for revealing His secrets to the childlike (Lk 10:21); exhorts His disciples to adopt their attitudes of humility, trust, and hope (Mt 18:3); and threatens severe punishment for anyone who would harm or take advantage of these little ones (Mt 18:6). Several times in the Gospel we see Jesus moved by the plight of sick children to heal them.

Here, a royal official, having heard of Jesus's visit to Cana, came from some twenty miles away to ask Jesus for help. His son was gravely ill, but Jesus's reputation inspired hope for healing. When Jesus hesitates, we can feel this man's desperation: "Sir, come down before my child dies!"

It is moving to see someone in a position of authority make themselves little before God in prayer. Even the rich and powerful experience hardships and tragedy. They too, need Jesus.

Every parent has known moments of powerlessness when their child was suffering or in danger. The stress even increases as children age, since teens and young adults can make mistakes with weighty consequences.

We can use this petition to pray for children and young people in need: "Lord, come down before my child dies!"

REMEMBER, LORD, the infant who leapt in the womb at Your presence and the innocents of Judea who testified by their blood at Your coming.

Remember the child whose offering You used to feed thousands and the little girl and the young man who were the first to experience Your power to raise us even from the dead.

Remember all those children whom You healed and blessed and the children of Jerusalem who acclaimed You as the Messiah.

Have mercy on those infants whose lives are cut short and on those who lose their parents. Have mercy on children who are abused and neglected; on those who suffer war and trauma; on those who are bullied or depressed.

Today, good Lord, I entrust to Your care this child in need, [name] whom You have created and blessed. Grant him/her your protection and an influx of new life. Do not allow him/her to perish but grant that he/she might grow in wisdom, age, and grace.

Please, Lord, come down quickly before my child dies. +

"Lord, give us this bread always" (Jn 6:34)[15]

John's Gospel does not describe the *institution* of the Eucharist but gives something just as precious. His account of the multiplication of loaves is followed by the "Bread of Life" discourse that enriches the Church's *theology* of the Eucharist.

The large crowd of pilgrims that came in search of Jesus the day after the multiplication of loaves was still motivated by the promise of earthly bread (Jn 6:20–26). "But man hungers for more. He needs more. The gift that feeds man as man must be greater, must be on a whole different level" (Pope Benedict XVI).[16]

Jesus does not disdain our basic needs but has something far greater to give: "You are looking for me . . . because you ate the loaves and were filled. Do not work for the food that perishes but for the food that endures for eternal life . . ." (Jn 6:26–27). Christ then reveals Himself as the "bread of God" come down from heaven to give life to the world (Jn 6:33). These mysterious words awakened a deeper hunger in the crowd: "Sir, give us this bread always" (Jn 6:34).

Ultimately, the human heart longs for fullness of life, love, and lasting communion. These goods, Jesus answers, are all given freely in the "Bread of Life," the offering of His very flesh for the life of the world. "Lord, give us this bread always."

HEAVENLY FATHER, You provided a garden for our first parents and manna for Your people in the desert. Your bread strengthened Elijah for forty days, and for the widow her flour and oil never failed.

You promised green pastures for Your sheep and a sumptuous banquet in heaven.

Your Son fed thousands with a few loaves, filled the nets of tired fishermen, and saved the very best wine for last.

To this day, You bless the earth, make it fertile, and supply the world with its grain.

And yet, my soul hungers not for signs or prophecies, neither choice wines nor bread in abundance but rather for the Bread of Life that is Your Son. His sacred Body is the only food, His precious Blood the only drink for a soul that longs for You.

Incline my heart to treasure the gift of the Eucharist and to never take it for granted; to long for You ardently, to thank You abundantly, and to adore You devoutly.

Lord, give us this bread always. +

"Lord, he whom you love is ill" (Jn 11:3)[17]

John's Gospel gives unique insight into the mystery of divine love. The eternal love between the Father and the Son is not only *revealed* but also *extended* to believers: God loves us with the love He has for the Son; Jesus's love for us flows from the Father's love for Him; and by loving one another, disciples remain in Jesus's love. John alone teaches that love touches God's very essence (1 Jn 4:8).

Since all that may sound beautiful but perhaps a bit abstract, John also observes that Jesus has a special love for individuals. John knew himself to be especially loved by Jesus (Jn 13:23, etc.), but this divine intimacy was not exclusive. John also notes that Jesus invited all His disciples to divine friendship (Jn 15:13) and that He loved Mary, Martha, and Lazarus (Jn 11:5).

The pain of Mary and Martha at their brother's death is something to which we can all relate. Their faith in God and in Jesus must have made it especially confusing that Christ would allow this to happen. Still, their delicate petition and the ensuing dialogue show the sisters' unwavering trust in Jesus. They know He could save their brother but trust His judgment. Much like Mary at Cana, the sisters simply present the problem and leave Jesus free to act. We too can use this petition to intercede for those suffering from moral or physical illness, knowing that they are loved by Christ: "Lord, he whom you love is ill."

✠

FOR THOSE WHO are bed-ridden, in chronic pain, or who can no longer pray for themselves; for those who are isolated in institutions, without close friends or family, who feel alone in this world and see little value to their lives: Lord, the one whom You love is ill.

For those fighting for their lives and health, who endure difficult treatment and need Your strength; for those who are depressed, who struggle to move beyond some terrible loss or trauma and have lost the will to live: Lord, the one whom You love is ill.

For those held captive by addiction or other destructive behaviors, unable to stop by themselves and break the cycle of dependency; for those suffering from a deformed image of themselves or their sexuality, who misuse their bodies or seek affection in unfulfilling ways: Lord, the one whom You love is ill.

For myself, burdened by sin and vices that turn me away from God, offend others, and suffocate my hope and well-being, Lord, the one whom You love is ill. +

"We want to see Jesus" (Jn 12:21)[18]

Scripture, while revealing God's attributes and works, also underscores His *mystery*. God transcends the created world, and our natural capacities are insufficient to know and express who He is (Is 55:8–9, Jb 38–40, etc.). Still, this transcendence does not stop believers from desiring to know God's "name" (Gn 32), to see His "glory" (Ex 33), or to seek His "face" (Ps 27).

John's Gospel reaffirms that no man has ever seen God as He truly is (Jn 1:18, 6:46). And yet, the incarnate Word has made God known (Jn 1:18) and revealed His "name" (Jn 17:6). In Jesus, the faithful catch a glimpse of God's "glory" (Jn 1:14, 2:11, etc.) and "see" the Father (Jn 14:9). So, as amazing as it would be to meet the historical Jesus, the contemplation of God in Christ is the object of our hearts' deepest longing: "We want to see Jesus!"

This request is the only petition in this collection not addressed directly to Jesus. Some pious Gentiles had heard about Jesus and asked His disciples to meet Him. Even today, non-believers may ask us about our faith and expect to "see" something of Jesus's goodness and mercy reflected in our attitudes: "We want to see Jesus!"

St. John Paul II used this same petition to encourage young people to seek out Jesus: "The desire to see Jesus dwells deep in the heart of each man and each woman . . . allow Jesus to gaze into your eyes so that your desire to see the Light . . . may grow within you."[19]

GOD OF OUR SALVATION, You sent Your Son as "the Light of the world" to make You known, so that He might give eternal life to all who believe. He died and rose to gather into one Your children dispersed throughout the world.

Yet, to this day so many do not know Christ. Most have heard Jesus's name and something about Christianity, but that is not enough. Our world is crumbling under the weight of ignorance and sin. Silently they cry: "We want to see Jesus!"

Our young people are hungry for truth and authenticity. They have questions about life and our troubled world. They are sensitive to beauty and justice but can be disappointed by members of the Church. Inspire witnesses who can awaken their faith: "We want to see Jesus!"

Holy Father, we also long to see the face of Your Son whom we adore and serve—to hear His voice in Scripture and preaching, to rest in Him at communion and prayer, to see Him alive in the saints. We too want to see Jesus! +

ACCLAMATIONS AND PROFESSIONS OF FAITH

At every Mass, the Church uses John the Baptist's acclamation of Jesus to confess her Eucharistic faith: "Behold the Lamb of God who takes away the sins of the world . . ." (Jn 1:29). As inspired revelation, such phrases have greater theological depth than what their original speakers may have known.

John's Gospel contains several such acclamations that result from transformative experiences of Jesus. As His contemporaries come to perceive something of Jesus's divine mystery, as faith dawns in their hearts, it is as if we are witnessing, in real time, divine revelation illuminate the minds of these people. Moved by the Holy Spirit (cf. 1 Cor 12:3), they discover that Jesus is more than just a preacher or healer, and that discovery provokes a spontaneous confession.

Expressing one's faith out loud can be stimulating for ourselves and for others. St. Teresa of Avila encourages believers to make use of such short, vocal prayers. When recited slowly and lovingly, mindful of the divine person to whom we are speaking, God can use even simple prayers to raise us to Himself:

> *"To keep you from thinking that little is gained through a perfect recitation of vocal prayer, I tell you that it is very possible that while you are reciting the Our Father or some other vocal prayer, the Lord may raise you to perfect contemplation. By this means His Majesty shows that He listens to the one who speaks to Him."*[20]

Not all the following acclamations were addressed directly to God or Jesus. Nonetheless, as inspired revelations of Jesus's mystery, the faithful can use these professions as powerful prayers of praise and adoration, like the Church does during her Eucharistic liturgy.

"Behold the Lamb of God who takes away the sin of the world" (Jn 1:29)

The first acclamation of Jesus in John's Gospel is a revelation from John the Baptist that inspires Jesus's first disciples. The title "Lamb of God" would have evoked the Passover lamb, whose blood protected the faithful from death and whose flesh was eaten at Passover (Ex 12). However, a grown man hailed as the "Lamb" more likely recalled the Lord's Servant, who, like a lamb led to the slaughter (Is 53:7), would humbly surrender Himself to abuse and death for the justification of many (Is 53:8–12).

Beginning with an exhortation to "behold" Jesus, this acclamation is first an invitation to *contemplation*. The expression is used to draw attention to an impressive sight, like the renovated Temple (Mk 13:1) or an apparition (Mk 13:21). In John's Gospel, the same verb is used by the crowds moved to see Jesus weeping over Lazarus, "See how he loved him!" (Jn 11:31); by Pilate presenting Jesus to the crowds, "Behold your king!" (Jn 19:14); and by Jesus inviting Thomas to examine His glorified body (Jn 20:27). With this same acclamation, "behold," the Baptist invites us to contemplate with gratitude our Savior come in the flesh.

In heaven, the saints behold the triumphant Lamb, offering Him praise and worship (Rev 5:6–14); He shines as their "lamp" for all eternity (Rev 21:23). That celestial worship and contemplation is anticipated at every Mass, when the priest presents the consecrated Body of Christ for the adoration of the faithful: "Behold the Lamb of God, who takes away the sin of the world!"

FORGIVE ME, LORD, for the many times when I am lethargic and dull of spirit. In Your mercy, send a prophetic voice from heaven to rouse my soul.

When I have fallen into sin and despair, turn my eyes with hope to the Redeemer who makes all things new: "Behold the Lamb of God!"

When I am saddened by injustice in the world or by the unpleasant, human side of the Church, remind me from Whom we have come and to Whom we are going: "Behold the Lamb of God!"

When I am distracted at Mass or disengaged from the liturgy, awake my soul and call my attention to the Holy One in our midst giving Himself as priest and victim on the altar: "Behold the Lamb of God!"

At the hour of my death, when regret for the harm I've done and the good I've neglected weighs heavily upon me, lift up my spirit with unshakeable hope to the One whose blood purifies from sin and Who loved me first: "Behold the Lamb of God!" +

"We have found the Messiah!" (Jn 1:41)

Several Gospel parables evoke the special joy that comes from *finding* something precious we have sought (cf. Lk 15:1–32). Many saints consider the dynamic of seeking and finding to be an ongoing part of the spiritual life. St. Gregory of Nyssa states, "Finding God means to seek him continuously."[21] St. Gregory the Great adds, "The Bridegroom [God] hides when he is sought, so that, not finding him, the Bride [our soul] may seek him with a renewed ardor."[22] St. John Paul II explains that the mystery of Christ is so great that this spiritual seeking will last our entire lives.[23] Jesus encourages this attitude among believers: "Seek and you will find . . ." (Mt 7:7).

John's Gospel tells us that Jesus's first disciples had been in the desert with John the Baptist preparing for the long-awaited Messiah. We can only imagine their joy when Christ had finally come. Their seeking led to divine intimacy when Jesus invited them to stay with Him (Jn 1:39). St. Thomas Aquinas describes as a "blessed day" such life-changing encounters with Christ.[24] Meeting Jesus sparked the disciples' desire to share their joy with others: "We have found the Messiah!"

This gospel acclamation is thus an act of Christian *witnessing*. Sharing the positive impact that Christ has had on our life is a simple, effective form of evangelization that does not require Holy Orders or advanced studies. Our living encounters with Christ in prayer and the sacraments can move us to bear witness: "We have found the Messiah!"

HEAVENLY FATHER, You so loved the world that You gave Your Only Son, so that everyone who believes in Him might have eternal life. But to believe in Him, they must know Him, and to know Him, they need witnesses who manifest that we have found the Messiah! So, Lord, we pray . . .

For lay missionaries, volunteers, and Catholics in the workplace—inspire in them the concrete works of service and witness that spread the life of Christ throughout the world.

For married couples and families—may their bonds of love and sacrifice build up domestic churches where charity is lived and faith is shared.

For consecrated persons—may the testimony of their vows, prayer, and fraternal life manifest the joy of Gospel-living and the beauty of friendship with Christ.

For the clergy—may their ministry of the Word and the sacraments make Christ present in our midst, lovingly teaching, governing, and sanctifying His people.

Together, through our charity and unity, may the world know: We have found the Messiah! +

"You are the Son of God, the King of Israel" (Jn 1:49)

Two words were all it took to convince Philip to leave everything and follow Jesus (Jn 1:43). However, it would take a bit more to motivate his friend Nathanael. Philip couches his confession of Jesus as the one foretold by Moses and the prophets (Jn 1:45), but Nathanael remains skeptical, "Can anything good come from Nazareth?" (Jn 1:46). When Jesus displays supernatural knowledge of his character and whereabouts (Jn 1:48), Nathanael is amazed.[25] Doubt gives way to faith, and Nathanael acclaims Jesus: "You are the Son of God, the King of Israel!"

For John and believers down the centuries, those messianic titles reveal more than what Nathanael knew at the time. Jesus is not simply "son of God" or "king of Israel" like David. Jesus is the Father's eternal Son (Jn 1:14), dwelling in His bosom (Jn 1:18) and sharing in His glory before the world began (Jn 17:5). His kingdom comes from God and is universal; He reigns in everyone who seeks the truth (Jn 18:36–37). Enthroned in heaven, He is the "Lord of lords and King of kings" (Rev 17:14).

When doubts darken our mind, Nathanael's confession reminds us that Christ knows us through and through. He speaks the language of our hearts and enlightens our minds with truths of faith that reach well beyond our limited understanding. He becomes our King, the more we listen to His voice and keep His word. May He reign over our hearts and in our world: "You are the Son of God and the King of Israel!"

LORD JESUS, soldiers gave You a crown of thorns and robe of crimson; they knelt in mockery before You and hailed You as king. Pilate's inscription proclaimed Your kingship as the crime for which You were condemned.

After two millennia, what has become of Your kingdom? Your name is known throughout the world, but who keeps Your word or obeys Your commands? How many kneel at Your name or honor You as Lord? Is there a country left in which Gospel values are the law of the land?

I submit to You, Lord, my heart, mind, and body. May my lips praise You, my vigor serve You, my heart adore You, and my sufferings unite me to You. I surrender to Your care my family, community, and country. May Your will and truth guide our actions and values.

And reign, Lord, over the Holy Land You once called home. May peace and justice return to peoples in conflict, as a light for the nations. You are the Son of God and the King of Israel! +

"Now we know that he is indeed the Savior of the world" (Jn 4:42)[26]

When we hear about the heroic deeds of the saints, we may have the impression that our own spiritual lives, comparatively modest, are of little importance to the Church. The conversion of a Samaritan village (Jn 4:39–42) reminds us of the potential impact of a simple act of witnessing.

Inspired by her transforming encounter with Jesus, the Samaritan woman ran off to share with her townspeople what had happened. St. Thomas Aquinas praises her clever preaching strategy: sharing what Jesus had done for her, leaving open the question of His identity, and inviting others to meet Jesus for themselves: "Come see a man who told me everything I have done. Could he possibly be the Messiah?" (Jn 4:29).[27] The townspeople who met Jesus were so enthused they invited Him to stay with them. Thus, a seed of truth sown in the heart of one woman led to an abundant harvest of faith: "We no longer believe because of your word: for we have heard for ourselves, and we know that this is truly the Savior of the world" (Jn 4:42).

When we have the privilege to preach or witness, the goal is not to impress people or attract them to ourselves, but rather to spark their encounter with Christ. We can all recall a gesture, a piece of advice, a testimony or homily that awakened our faith and placed us in contact with the Living God. When will it be our turn to witness? "Now we know that he is indeed the Savior of the world!"

GOD OUR FATHER, You sent Your Son to enlighten everyone in the world and Your Spirit to guide the Church in all truth.

Like the Samaritans and so many other lost sheep, we too who were once far off have been brought near to You through the saving mission of Christ.

Be praised, Lord, for the apostles and evangelists whom You sent as witnesses to the ends of the earth. Receiving their words as the word of God, we can profess the same faith: "Now we know that he is indeed the Savior of the world!"

Be praised for the early martyrs and fathers, for the mystics and doctors, and for the holy men and women of every era who have taught, practiced, and preserved for us a living heritage.

For our parents and elders, for the many priests and witnesses who patiently taught and corrected us so that we too might grow in age, wisdom, and grace, we thank You and confess: "Now we know that he is indeed the Savior of the world!" +

"Lord, to whom shall we go? You have the words of eternal life" (Jn 6:68)[28]

The "Bread of Life" discourse (Jn 6:22–59) was the first major challenge faced by Christ's disciples. Jesus's teaching was so surprising that "many" left Him that very day (Jn 6:66). That His flesh and blood must be eaten and drunk to have eternal life (Jn 6:58) was shocking, especially for Jewish sensibilities (Jn 6:60). The disciples struggled to assent to a teaching they did not understand.

At times we may also be troubled by a passage of Scripture or a decision by the Holy See. As cultural values shift, some teachings or disciplines can seem obscure to our human reason. What is a holy response to situations like these?

Catholics are asked to maintain a religious submission of will and intellect to the authentic magisterium of the Church.[29] Personal conscience needs to be informed by reliable sources and is not alone an authority for deciding the truth of a doctrine.[30] Involuntary doubt is the hesitation to believe and the persistent difficulty to resolve objections to the Faith. In such cases, we are invited to assent to revealed truths, while praying for enlightenment and actively striving to better understand them.[31]

In John's narrative, Peter is inspired to take a stand on behalf of the troubled disciples who wished to remain with Jesus. Peter's courageous profession (Jn 6:68) illustrates his role as "Rock" of the Church. We can find consolation in moments of trial by using this verse to reaffirm our apostolic faith: "Lord, to whom shall we go? You have the words of eternal life!"

LORD, I OFFER YOU this day the full assent of my intellect and will to every truth communicated for our salvation. Freely You chose to share with Your friends what You had seen and heard from the Father. Your words are spirit and life.

I also welcome, with faith and gratitude, the mediation of the apostles and their successors: "Whoever listens to you, listens to me . . ." I promise to receive the teachings of Your Church with reverent docility.

Please continue the merciful work of guiding my soul on the days when my faith is challenged.

When doubts overshadow my mind or my discernment is clouded by self-interest; when I can't make sense of some teaching and feel compelled to disagree; when a decision seems contrary to cherished traditions, or when I'd like to see a change that doesn't come,

Let Your good Spirit guide me to level ground and console my troubled soul. And let my heart confess with filial trust: "Lord, to whom shall we go? You have the words of eternal life!" +

"Yes, Lord. I have come to believe that you are the Messiah, the Son of God, the one who is coming into the world" (Jn 11:27)

Martha of Bethany, who makes this confession, is a friend of Jesus and an exemplary figure in John's Gospel. Addressing Christ as "Teacher" and "Lord" shows she is a disciple of Jesus.[32] She is confident and comes to Him with her concerns. She practices the service and hospitality He calls for (Jn 13:15–20). She remains docile in a tragic moment and maintains trust even when disappointed.

Jesus's delayed response to the sisters' plea to come and heal their brother was undoubtedly perplexing. Still, Martha does not dwell on the disappointment but immediately reaffirms her trust (Jn 11:22). Initially, she understands Jesus's promise that Lazarus will rise as referring to an event to come on Judgment Day (Jn 11:24). Then, Jesus reveals something new. The eternal life He has come to give begins *now*, not in some distant future; this supernatural life will continue beyond natural death (Jn 11:25–26).

Martha welcomes this revelation, even if she does not grasp it entirely. Instead of echoing back the Master's *lesson*, she wisely adheres to His *person*, "Yes, Lord. I have come to believe . . ." (Jn 11:27).[33] When faced with a trying situation or a mystery beyond our grasp, we too, like Martha, can say: "Lord, I adhere to Your teaching, because I trust *in You*."

The last phrase of her confession is striking, given that Jesus is standing right there: "You are . . . the one who is coming into the world." Martha has discovered that Jesus's salvific work is slowly unfolding before her and confidently surrenders to it.

LORD JESUS, I trust in You, and I will not stop trusting, even when my prayers do not seem to be answered as I hoped. To this day, You have showered me with "grace upon grace," and I do not doubt that will continue.

At present, I am troubled and entrust to Your care [name the concern]. I don't understand what is happening or what good can come of this. But with You at my side, I shall not fear. You have come to bring us life to the full, even here, even now.

You promised Martha that "if you believe, you will see the glory of God." I believe, Lord, and patiently await the dawning of that glory. May this situation not end in tragedy or death but lead to glory and life.

Am I sad and worried? Yes, but You are the resurrection and the life! Do I believe? Yes, Lord, I have come to believe that You are the Christ, the Son of God, the one who is coming, even now, into this world. +

"My Lord and my God!" (Jn 20:28)

The encounter between the apostle Thomas and the Risen Christ is a dramatic climax to John's Gospel and a bridge to our own experience. Thomas was absent on the evening of Easter Sunday when the Risen Lord appeared to the other apostles (Jn 20:24). John casts no blame on Thomas for this absence, so we are not to assume he was at fault. Instead, this trial was permitted by God for Thomas's sake and ours.

When the others share what happened while Thomas was away, he reacts with stubborn skepticism (Jn 20:25). Rather than trusting in the testimony of his brethren, Thomas announces his own criteria for confirming that Jesus had, in fact, risen from the dead: "Unless I see the mark of the nails . . . I will not believe" (Jn 20:25). His refusal to believe based on eyewitness testimony runs contrary to a major theme of John's Gospel. In general, we don't have direct experience of divine realities (Jn 1:18, 6:46) but must instead *believe* based on witnesses, like Jesus (Jn 3:11, etc.), the Baptist (Jn 1:6–8,15, etc.), and the beloved disciple (Jn 19:35, 21:24). In this way, Thomas represents future Christians who, like ourselves, have never met the historical Jesus but choose to believe based on apostolic testimony preserved in Scripture and Tradition.

Jesus mercifully accommodates Thomas's demands, corrects his unbelief, and proclaims blessed those who believe without empirical proof (Jn 20:27–29). Humbled by the encounter, Thomas professes his faith (Jn 20:28), helping us to overcome the temptation of holding God to our own criteria.

MERCIFUL LORD, thank You for coming to find me every time I stray into doubt or obstinacy. I do believe, Lord. Help my weak faith. Let every communion, every confession, every hour of adoration put me in contact with Your glorified body and call out to my soul:

"Here I am among you, especially in communities dedicated to me. I pass through locked doors, tense silences, and painful stalemates. I give you my peace and my Spirit. I am the door that no one can shut. I am the Resurrection and the Life!

"Here I am in all my priests just waiting to forgive. My breath will fill them, my wounds will heal you, and my words will lift you up again. I am the Good Shepherd of your soul!

"Here I am in the loving silence of the Eucharist. My sacred body is the light you seek, the proof you request, and the rest for which you long. Reach out your hand and respond with faith: 'My Lord and my God!'" +

"It is the Lord!" (Jn 21:7)

Although they are often hidden, contemplative souls are of great benefit to the Church. St. Thomas Aquinas teaches that contemplation should be shared with others.[34] Reflecting on the exchanges between John and Peter in the Gospel, Aquinas states that contemplatives (like John) should explain divine things to those busy with active ministries (like Peter). Contemplatives more readily recognize the mysteries of Christ, as John did at the tomb (Jn 20:8). He had a special charism for perceiving Jesus's divinity through the sensible signs of his humanity, which he then shared with the Church as evangelist.[35]

The closing chapter of John's Gospel gives us a good example of this: Simon had invited a few disciples for a night of fishing, but as dawn broke the group was still empty-handed (Jn 21:3). A stranger called out from the shore promising a catch if only they would cast on the right side of the boat. Obeying the strange order, their haul of fish was so great they could hardly pull it in (Jn 21:6). This unexpected abundance unleashed by obedience to a friendly word triggered the beloved disciple's perceptive faith: "It is the Lord!"

Remembering the past works of the Lord (Ps 77:11; cf. Mt 5:1–11) helps us to remain alert to His actions in the present. By sharing his perceptive faith, John teaches us to recognize Jesus at work in our lives, to see Him with the eyes of the heart, and to readily share that faith with others, "It is the Lord!"

BE BLESSED, O CHRIST, beloved Son of the Father, for the charism and holiness of Your beloved disciple John. By drawing close to You in friendship, he was graced to know You intimately and to contemplate Your mysteries. Grant that I may share in his devoted love and perceptive faith, so that I might recognize Your action in and around me:

To see and adore You in the most holy sacrament of the altar and there find rest for my soul: "It is the Lord!"

To appreciate You at work in those who serve faithfully, from pastoral care to domestic chores: "It is the Lord!"

To welcome with gratitude Your mother as my own, receiving her as your gift from the Cross: "It is the Lord!"

To remain united to You in moments of agony and so welcome new life springing from places of pain and death: "It is the Lord!"

To heed Your voice from the shore in moments of fruitless toil and so experience Your providential care: "It is the Lord!" +

"Lord, you know everything; you know that I love you" (Jn 21:17)

Jesus recognized Simon's potential at their first encounter. Renaming him "Cephas" (rock), the Lord began to forge in him the humble strength Peter would need to lead the Church. Jesus chose as the base of His ministry Peter's village of Capernaum (Jn 2:12; Mt 4:13), where He also gave His "Bread of Life" discourse. When that discussion caused many to desert Jesus, Peter's first act of leadership was to publicly profess his faith (Jn 6:68–69).

Peter would then be humbled. At the Last Supper, he was not seated at Jesus's right side (Jn 13:23–25),[36] and his promise of loyalty was met with a prophesy of future denial (Jn 13:36–38). His self-assured strength was corrected at Jesus's arrest (Jn 18:11) and failed him in the courtyard of the high priest, when Peter shamefully denied ever knowing Jesus (Jn 18:25–27).

Despite this failure, Jesus gave Peter several signs of renewed trust. He would administer God's mercy, care for Jesus's flock, and even die a martyr. Before that mission could begin, Jesus wanted to give Peter the opportunity to profess his love anew.

We too have fallen many times, despite our best intentions. We know well our weakness of will and need for God's grace. Like Peter, we would never claim to love Jesus "more than the others." This self-knowledge has come at the price of painful humiliations. We can use Peter's confession to express both contrition and gratitude: "Lord, you know everything; you know that I love you."

I PRAISE YOU, Lord, the Rock of my salvation. Creatures come and go, sentiments fade, and even promises last but for a time; You alone remain, sure and steadfast, just and faithful, without beginning or end.

You know the hearts of men and measure our souls at a glance. Patiently, You've heard my promises to change. You know my desire for holiness and efforts at conversion. Like wild flowers, they sprout quickly but wither under the heat of day.

And still, You choose me. To my wonder and gratitude, You call my name. Freely You give me new life and guide me back to Yourself when I stray. Knowing full well my capacity to falter, You shower me with graces. Time and again, You have restored me to Your friendship.

So today, having again offended You, I humbly ask not only for forgiveness but also for the grace to love You more fully, more faithfully. "Lord, you know all things; you know that I love you." +

GESTURES OF REVERENCE AND DEVOTION

Reverence and devotion for God can be powerfully communicated without use of words. In John's Gospel, the expression of "the greatest love" is not a poetic declaration but rather the *act* of "laying down one's life" for those whom He loves (Jn 15:13). The verb John chooses here (τίθημι "to lay down") elsewhere describes Jesus Himself freely "laying down his life" for His "sheep" (Jn 10:11–15) and in loving obedience to the Father (Jn 10:17–18). This supreme gesture of laying down one's very life out of love is also symbolized when Jesus, who "loved his own to the end" (Jn 13:1), solemnly "laid down" His outer garments at the Last Supper (Jn 13:4).

St. Thomas Aquinas reminds us that, as creatures endowed with both spirit and feeling, it is fitting for us to pray not only with the mind but also with the body, using sacred gestures like sacrifice, to express adoration.[37] Such exterior acts incarnate an interior offering of the soul to God. Liturgical theologian Romano Guardini adds that gestures of worship are "a form of speech by which the plain realities of the body say to God what its soul means and intends."[38]

John's Gospel records several gestures that can inspire Christian prayer. Jesus Himself lifts His eyes to heaven (Jn 11:41, 17:1) turning believers toward God. Discovery of Jesus's mercy and mystery provokes in many Gospel characters a response of love and reverence for Christ. Since the Word became flesh, worship "in Spirit and truth" no longer depends on the Temple but is centered on the "sanctuary" of Jesus's body (Jn 4:21–23; 2:21). Thus, gestures of devotion and reverence directed toward Jesus's humanity are now part of the "true worship" awaited by the Father (Jn 4:23).

Believers can use gestures narrated in John's Gospel to nourish their own piety and prayer, by making the interior acts of devotion and reverence embodied in those revealed gestures.

"And they remained with him that day" (Jn 1:39)[39]

—Abiding—

The first gesture of devotion toward Jesus in John's Gospel may appear unimpressive. To "stay put" in one place sounds lifeless and inert, like a stubborn stain on the wall. However, in John's vocabulary, to "remain" or "abide" (*menein*) expresses a core act of Christian spirituality.

For John, "abiding" describes first the mystery of the Trinity, a communion of love so complete that Jesus, the Spirit, and the Father are said to "be" and "dwell" in each other (Jn 1:32–33, 14:10, 17:21–23, etc.). Abiding also describes God's presence and action in believers: Jesus dwells in and with His disciples (Jn 6:56, 15:4–5), as does the Spirit (Jn 14:17) and even the Father (Jn 14:23). Finally, "abiding" is also a calling—disciples are to "remain" in Jesus and in the Father by staying faithful to His word and His love (Jn 8:31, 15:9–10) until the day when each will enjoy a "dwelling" in the Father's house (Jn 14:2).

Thus, when Jesus's first disciples answered His invitation by "remaining with him that day" (Jn 1:39), that gesture opened the door to a new form of communion beyond simply spending time at Jesus's earthly lodging. A true disciple, for John, is someone who "abides" with Jesus, i.e., keeps His word, stays faithful to Him, rests in Him, and shares in His loving communion with God. It is thus an act we are responsible for and a grace we are given. Jesus *wants* this abiding for His beloved disciples (cf. Jn 21:23), and the saints experience it in prayer.

"O my God, Trinity whom I adore," without beginning, without change, remaining forevermore; Each of You giving, each receiving life and love. Each One living in and glorifying the others, as the beloved lives in the lover.[40]

Your blessed life—to abide!

O Eternal Word and Beloved Son, come among us in the flesh, You promise: "I will not leave you orphans . . . I am with you always until the end of the age." Visitors pass by, sentiments run dry, yet You remain in the Host, present and hidden; body, soul, and divinity, totally given.

Your enduring mission—to abide!

O Sacrament Most Holy, may I truly adore You, rest on Your heart, contemplate, and console You. The flesh is weak, and hearts drift from You. May Your word, Your Spirit, Your presence keep me before You.

My desire, my vocation—to abide! +

"[The blind man] said 'I do believe, Lord' and worshipped him" (Jn 9:38)

—Worshipping—

In the Gospel, people who meet Jesus did not yet have the benefit of apostolic teaching and centuries of theological meditation. Initial faith moved them to welcome Jesus as the promised Christ and Savior, even without grasping His full mystery, as it would later be understood.

Thus, gestures of veneration directed at Jesus are rare in the Gospel. People seeking healing occasionally knelt before Him in homage and supplication. On rare occasions, a display of divine power moved Jesus's disciples to more profound reverence, like when he commanded the sea (Mt 14:33), rose from the dead (Mt 28:9), or ascended into heaven (Lk 24:52).

A striking example of this deeper reverence is offered to Jesus by the man born blind (John 9). His story is used to instruct catechumens, because it features a conversion from spiritual "blindness" to "seeing" Jesus in the light of faith. Despite public pressure to denounce Jesus as a charlatan, the man deduces from his cure that Jesus is "from God." The narrative climax occurs when Jesus reveals to him that he has "seen" the "Son of Man" in the flesh. The man reacts by professing his faith both in word and gesture: "'I do believe, Lord,' and he worshipped him" (Jn 9:38).

The ways in which Jesus has touched our own lives may often not be as dramatic as this miracle, but faith in Christ as Lord and Savior has also dawned in our hearts. Awareness of His holiness and divinity inspires gestures of reverent worship.

LORD JESUS, You came into our world to enlighten everyone, and in heaven You shine forever as the lamp of the blessed.

On the day of my baptism, You cleansed me and bestowed the light of faith. Time and again, You have ventured into the dark corners of my life, sowing seeds of truth, unmasking hidden lies, and enlightening my heart. By You, I've been washed; by You I can see. It has become my joy to worship You.

When questions arose in my heart, You patiently guided. Through searching and error, You stayed at my side. By mentors and failures, You taught and chided. You are the way and the end, my truth and my Savior. It is my joy to worship You.

What I believed then is now deeply known. So let me believe more firmly, until the day when believing becomes knowing, and knowing becomes sight. Your face unveiled will be my delight, and by the rays of Your infinite light, it will be my joy to worship You. +

"And the house was filled with the fragrance of the perfume" (Jn 12:3)[41]

—Anointing—

Following Lazarus's miraculous return to life, his family hosted a dinner party to honor Jesus (Jn 12:2). While Martha channeled her gratitude into service, we find her sister Mary at Jesus's feet, a posture of reverence familiar to her (Jn 11:32; Lk 10:39).

During the meal, Mary took a Roman pound of expensive perfume (about twelve fluid ounces or one-third of a liter) and poured it over the feet of Jesus.[42] The gift expresses loving devotion, while wiping his feet with her hair (a woman's "glory", 1 Cor 11:7) manifests her humility. Only servants were expected to handle a master's feet. If kings and guests of honor could be anointed on their heads, Mary's choice to anoint Jesus's feet attests to His supreme dignity in her eyes. John notes that the nard was "costly" (Jn 12:3), and Judas calculates its worth at three hundred days' wages (Jn 12:5).

Mary's lavish gesture reveals how precious Jesus's presence is for His closest friends. Just as her finest perfume was "kept" for such an occasion (Jn 12:7), so too we instinctively reserve the best of our time, talents, and ornaments to honor Christ in worship. John recalls how the whole house "was filled with the fragrance of the perfume" (Jn 12:3), reminding us how acts of loving devotion can transform our own lives and communities. An extravagant amount of spices was also used for Jesus's burial (Jn 19:40), again attesting that the body of Christ is worthy of our greatest human treasures.

"Take, Lord, and receive . . . all I have and call my own."[43] *My time and talents, energy and creativity; any kindness or spark of devotion; whatever there may be of value in me, it all comes from You, and I offer it now freely, a fragrant perfume to worship You.*

In the communion of saints, all the treasures of the Church are mine to share and enjoy. The heroic virtues of the saints and their loving acts of devotion; their tears of contrition and pearls of contemplation—may they permeate the house of my soul and radiate far and wide, a fragrant perfume to worship You.

The solitary prayers of an older priest and the fervent love of a young nun; fresh flowers for the tabernacle and hours spent in quiet adoration; the tireless care of a young mother and double shifts of a devoted father; warm hospitality for the poor, patient service to the sick, and attentive listening to those in distress—May these acts of charity anoint Your mystical body, a fragrant perfume to worship You. +

"There was reclining on Jesus' bosom one of His disciples, whom Jesus loved" (Jn 13:23)[44]

—Resting—

The most celebrated gesture of devotion in John's Gospel belongs to the beloved disciple who rested his head on Jesus's breast at the Last Supper. The scene assumes a seating arrangement typical in that period, with guests reclining on cushions disposed in a U shape around a low table, supporting themselves on their left elbows, and eating with their right hands.[45] The beloved disciple's position, sharing the central cushion with Jesus and immediately to His right, reflects his special favor. From there, he could easily lean back to rest "on Jesus' bosom" (Jn 13:23–25). Drawing close to the Lord in His sorrow reveals John's compassion and sensitivity to Jesus, who, in turn, entrusts John alone with the secret of the traitor (Jn 13:21–26).

For centuries, the ecclesial tradition has seen in this gesture a sign of mystical intimacy that can be experienced by other friends of Christ. For Origen, readers can reach a spiritual understanding of the Gospel if they become like "another John" who received sublime revelations while resting "in the bosom of the Word."[46] Other Fathers, like Ephrem and Jerome, view John as actively drawing from the breast of Christ the divine mysteries He later preached and taught.[47] Aquinas adds that those who, like John, draw closer to Christ and unite themselves to God in love, will receive secrets of divine wisdom.[48] John Paul II invites the faithful to spend time with Christ in Eucharistic adoration, lying close to the breast of Jesus like John and there drawing consolation.[49]

O Sacred Heart of Jesus, from Your fullness we have all received grace upon grace; Wellspring of living waters for the sanctification of souls, in You I take my rest.

O Sacrament Most Holy, what a blessing it is to adore You. One hour in Your presence is more restful than a thousand elsewhere. At Your feet concerns are pacified, intentions are received, and the heart settles. Through communion You draw us to Yourself, like branches on the vine. In You I take my rest.

O bosom of my Lord and Savior, refuge of the repentant and consolation of the distressed, from You I have received words of light and life, peace in times of conflict, and strength when trials abound. Your green pastures and still waters refresh the weary soul. In You I take my rest.

Grant, at the hour of my passing, to recline on You one last time, that from Your breast I may be drawn into the bosom of the Father and there, with and in You, find eternal rest. +

"Standing by the cross of Jesus . . ." (Jn 19:25)

— Standing—

Catholic piety holds in high esteem this verse from John's Gospel, partly due to the influence of the thirteenth-century hymn "Stabat Mater Dolorosa" still used in "Via Crucis" devotions.

Depictions of the Blessed Virgin fainting at the foot of the cross became popular during the late Middle Ages, but that tradition was soon corrected by theologians of the Counter-Reformation like Thomas Cajetan and Peter Canisius.[50] They pointed out that the Gospel does not describe Mary collapsing under the weight of sorrow. Instead, the evangelist repeats twice (Jn 19:25–26) that Mary and the beloved disciple remained standing near the Cross of Jesus. The Greek verb *histēmi* (to stand) was translated literally by the Latin Vulgate *stabant, stantem*, preserving this gesture in Western Christendom.

Remaining silent and upright at such a tragic moment suggests a heroic and steadfast faith: "Those trusting in the Lord are like Mount Zion, unshakeable, forever enduring" (Ps 125:1). The faith of Mary and John adhered to a divine mystery at work beneath the human tragedy of the crucifixion.

John notes elsewhere that a friend of Christ is someone who "stands and listens," awaiting the divine redeemer (Jn 3:29–31). This standing also anticipates the victory of the Lamb who "stands" in heaven (Rev

5:6, 14:1) and of the elect who "stand" before His throne (Rev 7:9). With fixed attention, Mary and John united themselves in faith and love to the oblation of Christ. May we also be granted to stand in hope when the cross appears in our lives.

TODAY, LORD, I DESIRE to take my stand in the shadow of Your holy Cross. Although every instinct urges flight, it is here that I was born, here that I am drawn, and here that I return, time and again, repentant and hopeful. Let me stray no longer but with You take my stand.

Here I can stand, because You are upright, a tower of mercy reaching up to heaven; because You are victorious over sin and death; because You breathed Your last, loving us to the very end. Leaning on You, cleaving to You; drawn, held, and saved by You, can I stand.

Today, I plant my feet beside the one You gave me as mother. Afflicted but not crushed, like one seeing the invisible, she stood firm. With her, I witness and receive the greatest love. A pillar of faith, a mountain unshaken, with her do I stand.

And so, by Your grace, at the hour of my death and on the day of Your return—redeemed and hopeful—Your glory triumphant, O Lord let me stand. +

"They put a sponge full of the wine on a branch of hyssop and held it to his mouth" (Jn 19:29)[51]

— Quenching —

Printed on the wall of every chapel of the Missionaries of Charity throughout the world are the words of Jesus crucified: "I thirst" (Jn 19:28). This phrase inspired the vocation of St. Mother Teresa of Calcutta, who devoted her life to responding to the thirst of Jesus by loving prayer and devoted service to the poor: "I belong to Jesus; I have been chosen, with a purpose to satiate His thirst for love by loving Him, by putting this love for Him in action."[52]

Some sixty years prior, those same words of Jesus also inspired St. Therese of Lisieux. An image of Christ crucified provoked her resolve "to remain in spirit at the foot of the Cross." She felt Jesus's cry of thirst "continually echoing in [her] heart," with a desire to quench Jesus's thirst: "I slaked His thirst and the more I gave Him *to drink*, the more the thirst of my poor little soul increased, and it was this ardent thirst He was giving me as the most delightful drink of His love."[53]

Since food and drink have a double, spiritual meaning elsewhere in John's Gospel (Jn 4:10, 4:34, 6:33, etc.), it seems likely that the object of Jesus's thirst was something more than the wine-vinegar offered to Him (Jn 19:29–30).[54]

What is Jesus asking for when He comes to the well of my soul asking for a drink (cf. Jn 4:7) or when He cries out His thirst from the cross? What could I offer Him in response?

For what do You thirst, Lord?

Today, I offer my adoration—may it be reverent and enduring; my praise—may it be joyful and sincere; my contrition—make it firm with resolve.

You, the Alpha and Omega, full of grace and truth, resting in the bosom of the Father and loved by Him before creation, possessing the Spirit and eternal glory, for what could You possibly thirst?

What I have is so little and unfitting—not frankincense, gold, or myrrh; not a pound of fine perfume; neither the innocence of a child, nor the virtue of the saints. The water of my words and works is always tainted with the vinegar of vice and sin.

Still, may whatever in me that is good be Yours, because all that is Yours is mine! A pure heart create in me, O God. By drinking, make it holy; by receiving, make it pleasing to You. May the living waters of Your grace, welcomed and returned with faith and love, in prayer and service, satisfy Your thirst, Lord. +

PRAYING WITH THE PRAYERS OF JESUS

Our foray into praying with John's Gospel will culminate with the prayers of Jesus Himself. While the other evangelists often describe Jesus retiring to pray or teaching His disciples about prayer, John lets us *hear* Jesus pray, providing the most extensive selection of Christ's prayers addressed to the Father.

In John's Gospel, Jesus prays not in solitary places but publicly and audibly. Those prayers are *revelatory*, allowing us to contemplate Christ's mystery as God's Only Son. They are also *sanctifying*, meant to draw us into His intimate relationship with God. In the Synoptics, Jesus introduces His disciples into a new way of relating to God by giving them the *Pater Noster*. In John's Gospel, Jesus illustrates what a filial relationship with God looks like by His own words and attitudes in prayer. Twice, we even see Him "raise his eyes to heaven" (Jn 11:41, 17:1) to pray, manifesting with His body the interior attitude of the Son eternally turned "toward" the Father (Jn 1:2–18).

"To pray," in John's spirituality, "is thus to allow oneself to be drawn up toward the Father by Christ . . . Prayer, for John, is a process of elevation that leads into the very mystery of Jesus" (Mollat).[55]

We see Jesus at prayer on five separate occasions in John's Gospel. Each prayer manifests something special about what it means to live as God's beloved children. The original meditations proposed in this section do not pretend to complete or elaborate on the perfect prayers of Christ. Rather, they are an attempt, however imperfect, to make Jesus's prayers our own, to adopt His filial attitudes and piety with words adapted to our condition as creatures and sinners. What better way can we "come to the Father" through Christ (Jn 14:6), than by praying with the very prayers of Jesus?

"Father, I thank you for hearing me. I know that you always hear me" (Jn 11:41–42)

This praise recalls an earlier prayer of Jesus. Having received five loaves of bread from a generous boy, Jesus "gave thanks" (Jn 6:11)—the same verb used at the Last Supper (Mt 26:27) which is the root of our word "Eucharist." Jesus's thanksgiving likely took the form of the customary blessing, "Blessed are you Lord, who bring forth the bread of the earth . . ."[56] It is striking that Jesus gave thanks for the child's meager offering *before* the miracle takes place.

A similar prayer of thanksgiving occurs before the raising of Lazarus. At the open tomb, Jesus lifts His eyes to heaven and says, "Father, I thank you for hearing me" (Jn 11:41). Apparently, Jesus had already addressed a silent petition to God, suggesting an ongoing dialogue between Him and the Father that was not always expressed.[57] Jesus then prays audibly so the miracle would be recognized as the joint work of the Father and the Son (Jn 11:42b).

Here, Jesus's filial piety shines. Because He seeks to please God in all things (Jn 8:29), Jesus *knows* that the Father always hears His prayers. From Him, we learn to thank God without seeing the results of our petitions, embracing Jesus's trust in the Father: "This is the confidence we have before him that if we ask anything according to his will, he hears us" (1 Jn 5:14).

Jesus also teaches us, even in moments of grief and loss, to surrender with trust to whatever God decides or permits: "Father, I thank you for hearing me . . ."

GRACIOUS FATHER, I thank You for hearing me and surrounding me so faithfully with Your loving care.

Generously and without fail, You supply my daily bread. For beauty and truth, friends and laughter, health and occasions to grow, I am grateful. Thank You for hearing me, even when I haven't thought to ask or paused to give thanks.

For providing the daily bread of my soul, the Eucharist that abides and gives life, and for the Scriptures, prayed and preached, that never fail to speak, correct, and strengthen, thank You for hearing me.

Daily I implore forgiveness, and Your mercy abounds. Daily I ask for guidance, and Your good Spirit leads. For consolation in distress and for light in dark times; for resistance in temptation and for protection from evil, thank You.

In all those who have helped, guided, and loved me far beyond my merit, I see the imprint of Your guiding hand and the contours of Your gentle face. Thank You, Father, for I know You always hear me. +

"Father, glorify your name" (Jn 12:28)

This prayer comes from a scene in John's Gospel that parallels Jesus's agony in the garden. The arrival of a few Gentile Greeks who wish to see Jesus signals that the "hour" of His "glorification" has finally come (Jn 12:23), i.e., when Jesus will accomplish God's saving plan and be "lifted up" into heavenly glory through the cross, thus obtaining eternal life for all who believe (Jn 12:32–33).[58]

Jesus knows well that accomplishing His mission will involve painful trials: the violent destruction of His own body (Jn 2:19), the betrayal of a chosen disciple (Jn 6:71), a final confrontation with Satan (Jn 12:31), and the loss of His own life (Jn 12:24). That He naturally recoils from such hardships underscores Jesus's full humanity and is something we can all identify with.

Although "troubled" by His impending Passion, Jesus overcomes the reflex to ask God to preserve Him from the trials ahead (Jn 12:27). Instead, His prayer, "Father, glorify your name" (Jn 12:28), manifests the "greater love" (Jn 15:13) that fills Jesus's heart. With this prayer, Jesus asks that God's will may triumph over any weakness or obstacles.

Even for people of faith, distressing situations may push us to make heartfelt supplications like "save me from this hour" (Jn 12:27) or "take this cup from me" (Mk 14:36). Those are authentic expressions of hope. But, as we entrust ourselves to Christ and implore His help, another prayer may quietly emerge, like the living waters of grace rising up through the cracks of stress and strain: "Not my will but thine . . . Father, glorify your name."

FATHER, BE CLOSE to me in this hour of trial. Into Your sure and steady hands, I entrust my soul.

When darkness surrounds me, and Your presence is but a memory that I cling to in faith; when prayer and Scripture turn dry and silent; when the usual sources of guidance seem obscure, and I feel all alone; come near, Father, and glorify Your name.

When the burden of sin overwhelms me, and I feel loathsome before You; when I don't even want to pray and prefer to drown out my pain with distractions; heal me, Father, and glorify Your name.

When fear and dread paralyze the soul, and my courage evaporates; when anxiety keeps me up at night and worries dominate my prayer; sustain me, Father, and glorify Your name.

At this hour, I need Your strength, for I am but flesh; I need Your light, for I can see and feel nothing; I need Your love, to choose the greater good. I cannot do this alone . . . but I am not alone. Father, glorify Your name! +

"Glorify your son . . . so that he may give eternal life to all those you have given him" (Jn 17:1–2)[59]

This petition opens chapter seventeen of John's Gospel, sometimes called "Jesus's High-Priestly Prayer," in which Christ solemnly intercedes for believers.[60] Jesus bares His heart, revealing the intentions He carried into His Passion and thus the very goods for which He freely accepted death. Jesus's prayer at this moment manifests how much we believers are part of His intimate relationship with the Father.

Amid distressing circumstances, Jesus's magnanimity shines through. His main concerns are *to glorify the Father* by accomplishing His work and making His mercy known to the world, and *to give life* to others by sharing with believers His blessed life as eternal Son.

By asking to be "glorified" by the Father, He is requesting that the Father bring about these goods through His Passion; that God's love for His Son and for humanity be seen to triumph over sin and death; that Jesus's self-offering be a means of divine glory for His humanity and of divine life for all those whom He carries in His sacred heart.

Glorifying God and giving life are also central to our mission as Christians. Professional success may be gratifying but cannot satisfy the heart's thirst to give and receive life and love. Baptism then endows us with new, spiritual life and the mission to share that new life. So, with the words of Jesus we can pray for the grace needed to carry out this vocation.

HOLY FATHER, You sent Your Son into the world to bring eternal life to all who believe. He left us His Spirit, His words of eternal life, and His own flesh as bread for the life of the world.

Along with those precious gifts, He also called us to give freely as we have received, to love as You love, and to bear much fruit for Your glory.

Good Father, I want nothing more than to embrace and to share the life of Your Son. Other forms of success matter little. I want to give Your life, light, and love. The hope of bearing good fruit gets me up in the morning. For that purpose, I labor and serve, listen and preach.

So, it pains me, Father, to feel useless, like a barren tree, a branch cut off, a dry, weary land. Most of my labors come to nothing. What do I still lack?

Glorify Your son/daughter, granting me the graces I need to carry out my mission, so that I may give life those entrusted to my care. +

"Holy Father, keep them in your name . . . so that they may be one" (Jn 17:11)

One detail about Christ's Passion is found only in John's Gospel. Having crucified Jesus, the soldiers divided His garments by tearing them into four equal parts. However, finding His tunic was seamless, woven in one piece from top to bottom, they preserved it whole (Jn 19:23–24).

Church Fathers like St. Cyprian saw in the Lord's tunic a symbol of the one Faith and one Church that has come down to us from heaven: "Undivided, united, and connected, it shows the coherent harmony of our people who put on Christ. By the sacrament and sign of this garment, he has declared the unity of the church."[61]

Jesus, in His solemn prayer to the Father before His Passion, prays three times for the unity of the faithful (Jn 17:11, 20–21, 22–23). This petition is so dear to Him that it concerns much of the prayer. For the sake of Christian unity, Jesus gave believers the "glory" of His Spirit and implores the Father to "keep them in [His] name."

Why is unity so important to Him? The communion of Jesus's disciples shares in the eternal bond of love between the Father, Son, and Holy Spirit. It is thus the visible manifestation of that invisible reality, and a sign of credibility before the world. Lack of charity among believers, conflict and rivalry between Christian communities, and divergent doctrines—all these send a confused message to the world and detract from our sharing in the mystery of God's love.

WE THANK YOU, FATHER, for the witness of loving Christian families. Help couples to remain faithful, blessing them with patience and tenderness. Grant families the acceptance and selfless love that is our first school of charity. That we may be one!

Bless our local parishes. Grant us the grace to welcome the diversity of Your flock and to be patient with each other's flaws. Teach us to be generous with our time and talents. Send us wise and devout pastors and help us to appreciate those whom You send. That we may be one!

Be praised for the institutes of consecrated life in our midst. Their witness, prayer, and service are a treasure. Bless them with authentic charity, a sign of fraternal love that we need to see. That they may be one!

Protect the universal Church spread throughout the world. Help us to cultivate and cherish, beyond our diverse cultures and traditions, the bonds of charity and the deposit of faith. Holy Father, keep us in Your name, that we may be one! +

"Father, they are your gift to me. I wish that there where I am they also may be with me, that they may see my glory" (Jn 17:24)

The final petition in Jesus's solemn prayer opens with a lovely phrase: "Father, they are your gift to me." It is touching to hear Jesus speak this way about His disciples. He does not retain how they were slow to understand, considered leaving, jostled for honors, or betrayed Him. We, too, have done plenty to disappoint Jesus, but what He sees when He looks upon His flock of believers is a "gift" from the Father.

Embracing that outlook on my brothers and sisters in the Faith will help transform my experience of Christian community. Countless times I have benefited from a welcoming smile, a word of wisdom, a rousing hymn or edifying homily. Even moments of friction have been places of growth in charity. God was there through it all, forging us in faith and love: "Father, they are your gift to me."

Christ then makes the stunning request that His followers might behold His divine glory. During Jesus's earthly ministry, the disciples caught glimpses of His glory through miracles as at Cana, or at rare moments like the Transfiguration. We also have learned to contemplate Jesus indirectly through revealed words and symbols and to be content with loving Him in the night of faith.

But Jesus wants more for us. He asks that we might dwell in His presence and behold His glory. In the perspective of John's Gospel, those future blessings already begin, perhaps in hidden ways, during this earthly life.[62]

"Father, they are your gift to me."

The saints who live out the Gospel; the doctors who fortify my faith; the caring pastors who guide, exhort, and listen; the consecrated who pray and serve; the married who incarnate love and transmit the faith; the devoted laity who edify our communities; the Church whom I need and love, they are all Your gift to me.

"That they also may be with me."

Place me, Father, with Your Son. I want to be there where He is, at Your side and in Your bosom; beloved under Your gaze and shining with Your glory.

Beneath the shadow of Your wings, shelter me. By Your gentle hand, guide me. As the apple of Your eye, keep me with Jesus.

"That they may see my glory."

Reveal to me the glory of Your Son, in the Gospel and the Eucharist; in my brothers, in our pastors, and in the poor;

In the darkness of faith and the warmth of communion; here on earth as in heaven, let me see His glory. +

"I thirst" (Jn 19:28)

This mysterious phrase is one of the seven last words of Jesus crucified.

Is it a *revelation* of divine longing addressed to humankind, a thirst to give life, love, and salvation ? Many saints across the centuries have read this verse in that way: It indicates "his intense desire for the salvation of the human race" (Aquinas);[63] "Are we truly seeking to satiate the thirst of God, our loving Father in heaven, for our holiness—the thirst which Jesus expressed on the cross?" (Mother Teresa).[64] Although God is perfect and lacks nothing, He bestows gifts out of love and for a salvific purpose that awaits our response.

Or is this phrase rather *a prayer* of Jesus addressed to God, expressing Christ's longing to accomplish God's will, to love and glorify Him (cf. Jn 4:34; 5:30; 17:1, etc.)?[65] Perhaps, Jesus, having embraced our condition as creatures, expresses in this prayer the human longing for communion with God, echoing other biblical prayers that cry out the thirst of a persecuted just man (Ps 22:16, 69:21) or the spiritual thirst for God (Ps 42:2–3; 63:1;143:6, etc.).

Both readings seem valid. For our purposes here, we can receive Jesus's phrase as a prayer and make it our own, expressing our thirst for God both in times of dryness and in moments of fervor. We can also use it to give voice to others' longing for God, especially those who do not know Him, who feel far from Him, or who are in urgent need of Him.

My God, You are the daily bread and living water I need to survive and to thrive. Without the gift of Your presence, I cannot pray. Without Your word alive within, my soul is numb. Without Your Spirit, I am ruled by disordered affections.

Come, then, and permeate the dry, weary land of my soul. You who came to find the lost and bring life in abundance, do not leave me to wander and wilt.

I thirst for Your light—to reveal new facets of Your mysteries and help me to discern with faith.

I thirst for Your love—to comfort the soul and make me caring and cheerful for others.

I thirst for Your word—to anchor my heart, nourish my prayer, and provide wisdom to share with others.

I thirst for Your mercy—to pick me up from the dust and restore the purity and joy lost by sin.

Father, I thirst with Jesus's thirst for You and for souls—that sinners may repent, that the lost may find You, and that those who know You may love You more. +

PART TWO

Praying to St. John the Evangelist

TRADITIONAL PRAYERS

I

Ancient Prayer to John the Theologian

St. John was praised as "the theologian" by Greek Fathers as early as the third century. The epithet means someone who has come to know God intimately and transmitted that graced knowledge to the benefit of others.

The following "apolytikion" (concluding hymn) is still chanted today (in its Greek original) by monks on Mount Athos and in Orthodox churches around the world. Its exact origin is unknown, but it may reach back into the patristic era, making this perhaps the oldest prayer to St. John.[66]

Beloved Apostle of Christ our God,
hasten to deliver a people without defense.

He who permitted you to recline upon His bosom,
accepts you on bended knee before Him.

Beseech Him, O Theologian,
to dispel the clouds of darkness that surround the world, asking for us peace and great mercy. Amen.

2

Praise for Saint John's Purity of Heart

St. Ephrem the Syrian (ca. 306–73) was a teacher and composer of liturgical hymns. This excerpt from "Hymn on Virginity XV"[67] is a baptismal prayer praising John the Baptist, John the Evangelist, and Peter. Strophes 4–5 honor St. John as virgin, beloved disciple, and theologian:

Blessed are you, chaste youth,
whom your Lord held like a child.

He loved and cherished you, chaste disciple,
in whom was hidden the pearl.

Virginity came down and lifted you up;
before onlookers, upon His breast He exalted you.

Blessed are you, enriched by love, the key
of the treasury you happened upon.

The treasury had never been opened;
silence was its seal, but your voice opened it.

Blessed is your mouth that composed for us,
"He is the Word."

You explained the silent word to satisfy us:

"God is the Word" a reality for the diligent,
an enigma for seekers. Amen.

3

An Ambrosian Hymn to John the Beloved

The first Christian hymns in Latin were composed during the fourth century by St. Hilary of Poitiers (d. 367) and Saint Ambrose of Milan (d. 397). Many Ambrosian-style hymns were composed over the fourth and fifth centuries, including beloved prayers still in use today like the "Te Deum."

This hymn from the Ambrosian breviary, for John "honored by the love of Christ," is still sung in its original Latin verse.[68]

Amore Christi nobilis,
Et filius tonitrui,
Arcana Ioannes Dei
Fatu revelavit sacro.

John, honored by the love
of Christ and named by
Him the Son of Thunder,
revealed in sacred words
the hidden things of God.

Captis solebat piscibus
Patris senectam pascere:
Turbante dum natat salo,
Immobilis fide stetit.

He was a fisherman and
supported his aged parent
by his toil: whilst sailing
on the troubled waves,
he received the faith, and
firmly did he hold to it.

Hamum profundo merserat, *Piscatus est verbum Dei:* *Iactavit undis retia,* *Vitam levavit hominum.*	He throws his hook into the deep and catches the Word of God; he lets down his nets into the waters and draws in Him who is the Life of men.
Piscis bonus pia est fides, *Mundi supernatans salum,* *Subnixa Christi pectore,* *Sancto locuta Spiritu.*	His fervent faith is the good fish which swam through the briny flood of this world; it rested on the breast of Christ and thus spoke in the Holy Spirit:
"In principio erat Verbum, *Et Verbum erat apud Deum;* *Et Deus erat Verbum:* *Hoc erat in principio apud Deum.*	"In the beginning was the Word, and the Word was with God, and the Word was God. The same was in the beginning with God.
"Omnia per ipsum facta sunt" *Sed ipse laude resonet,* *Et laureatus spiritu* *Scriptis coronetur suis.*	"All things were made by Him." Then, let us sing the praises of this Disciple, and since he bears the laurel of the Spirit, let his writings be his crown.

4

Ode to Saint John the Soaring Eagle

A learned philosopher and theologian from Ireland, John Scottus Eriugena (ca. 815–77) later served as the court theologian in Carolingian France. His homily on John's Prologue was one of the most widely read texts of its kind in medieval Europe. This short ode in praise of the evangelist sums up Eriugena's Johannine spirituality.[69]

With holy toil, you penetrate the secrets, O John, that no man, however sharp his mind or shining with highest wisdom, could ever reach by study, of when the eternal God made flesh was born of a virgin. And since you rose up beyond the stars on the wings of language, the symbol of an eagle soaring through the heavens is yours forever. Amen.

Cum sancto penitras arcana labore, Iohannes / Quae nullus potuit hominum nec mentis acumen / Alta sophia nitens unquam penitrare legendo / Ut Deus aeternus factus caro virgine natus; / Et quia verborum pennis super astra petisti, / Te species aquilae sequitur, quae pervolat ethra.

5

O John, Virgin Disciple So Dear

Bl. Notker the Stammerer (840–912) was a Benedictine monk from the abbey of St. Gall, Switzerland. A gifted poet, composer, and scholar, his eloquence overcame a life-long speech impediment for the praise of God.[70]

O John, virgin disciple so dear to Jesus,
You who, for His love, left your earthly father on the shore,
You who merited to drink from the sacred waters that flowed from His side,
You who, while on this earth, contemplated the glory of the Son of God,
A glory that none can see, we believe, except the saints in heaven,
You whom Christ, from his triumphant Cross, chose to care for His Mother,
We implore you: commend us to God by your fervent prayers, O John, the beloved of Christ.

Amen.

6

Hymn to John, Guide Most Sure

An Italian Benedictine monk later called to serve as bishop, St. Peter Damian (ca. 1007–72) labored to draw priests back to a prayerful, disciplined lifestyle. Read within that focus of his mission, this hymn for St. John's feast day may have provided clergy with a model of holy ministry and friendship with Christ.[71]

Worthy virgin guardian of the Virgin,
And faithful scribe of the eternal Word,
Erase the debts of your servants,
O Saint John.

Not hesitating, you left behind
Your earthly father to obey our Father in heaven,
Leaving fish for the new calling
Of catching myriads of men.

Flowing like a river from the eternal source,
You pour out living waters on the parched earth,
Overflowing from the breast of Christ
What your heart found in His.

Light from heaven and splendor on earth,
Obtain the forgiveness of all our wrongs,
And grant that we may plumb the depths
Of the mysteries you taught.

You who contemplated the Father's hidden Word,
Protect our faith from all error
And lead us toward the sweet vision to come,
O guide most sure.

Praise be to God the Father
And honor to his Only Begotten,
And to you, Holy Spirit, may constant zeal,
Resound from our mouths forever.

Amen.

7

Prayer to John in Times of Penance

From St. Anselm of Canterbury (1033–1109), we have perhaps the oldest collection of private prayers in Western literature. His two prayers to St. John reflect a deeply penitential spirit. The apostle's intimacy with Christ is believed to make him a powerful intercessor.[72]

Holy and blessed John,
chief of the evangelists of God,
and most beloved apostle of the Lord,

You were pre-eminent in the love of God
among so many who were eminently loved,
so that outstanding love was your
characteristic sign among them all.

John, who reclined regularly on the glorious
breast of the Most High, God gave you to His
mother as her son in place of Himself
when He left her at bodily death.

To you, blessed one,
so loving and so loved by God,
this poor man who stands guilty before God
appeals with prayers, so that by the
intercession of one so loved he may be spared
from God's just punishment.

For, sir, because of his sins
he needs someone to intervene for him,
and he runs to that well-known friendship of yours with God whose retribution he fears.

I know, sir, what power you have
through that same friendship by which you obtain from God whatever you ask.

John, John, if you are that disciple whom Jesus loved,
I pray you, by virtue of that same privilege,
let me, by your prayers,
be that sinner whom Jesus forgives.

If that glorious breast
was a familiar place for you to lean upon,
I ask that, through you, it may become for me a place of salvation.

Amen.

8

Praise to Share in John's Holiness

Adam of St. Victor (1112–46) was a composer and poet from the abbey of St. Victor in Paris which produced several renowned theologians of the High Middle Ages. His "Gratulemur Ad Festivum," excerpted here, draws together threads of the preceding Johannine tradition.[73]

Let us rejoice for the feast.
Let us be glad
for John's votive celebration.

Thus, let our praise be recited out loud,
that our heart is not cheated of the savor
by which it tastes joy.

This is one particularly beloved of Christ,
who, reclining on His breast,
drew wisdom from Him.

Christ on the Cross
commended to him His Mother.
This virgin, John, protected
her who did not know man.

He burns inside with charity,
and shines outside with purity,
by his signs and eloquence.

Writing the Gospel,
he bears the character of an eagle,
gazing at the ray of the sun,
namely [the divine] beginning,
the Word in the beginning.

By his writings, the unity of the Church is enlightened,
and enlightened,
it is strengthened.

Hail, vessel of sound purity,
vessel filled with heavenly dew,
clean inside, clear outside,
noble throughout.

Make us follow your holiness.
Cause us, through purity of mind,
to contemplate the Trinity,
one in substance.

Amen.

9

Prayer to the Lamb's Dearest Son

St. Hildegard of Bingen (1098–1179) was among the first of many medieval nuns to report visions of St. John. She believed to have shared in his charism as theologian in her own writing and composed two choral responsorials for his feast day, excerpted here:[74]

O mirror of the purest dove,
you gazed upon the mystical expanse
plunging into clear, living waters.

O wondrous, flourishing bloom
that never withered, never fell—
the heavenly Gardener sent you to tell.

O sweet repose of sunshine's embrace:
you the Lamb's dearest son,
who chose his friendship for a new fecundity.

O gentle chosen one,
inflamed by the Flame
you gleamed, and like a root
reaching into the Father's splendor,
you enlightened the mysteries.

Amen.

10

Prayer for Mary and John's Intercession

Named after its first words praising Mary's purity, the "O Intemerata" is an anonymous prayer to the Virgin Mary and the Apostle John. It was popular throughout the Middle Ages, with variations of the prayer appearing in liturgical books as early as the twelfth century. The following excerpt is taken from a fifteenth-century version.[75]

O unspotted and forever blessed, unique and incomparable virgin Mary, Mother of God, most graceful temple of God, sanctuary of the Holy Spirit, gate of the kingdom of heaven, by whom next unto God the whole world lives, incline O Mother of Mercy your ears of piety unto my unworthy supplications, and be merciful to me a most wretched sinner, and be unto me a helper in all things.

O most blessed John, the beloved and friend of Christ, which by the same Lord Jesus Christ was chosen a virgin, and among the rest more beloved, above all instructed in the heavenly mysteries, for you were made a most worthy Apostle and Evangelist: upon you also I call, together with Mary, the Mother of the same Lord Jesus Christ our Savior, that you would grant me your aid with hers.

O you two celestial jewels, Mary, and John. O you two lights divinely shining before God. Chase away by your bright beams the clouds of my offenses.

For you are those two in whom God the Father through His own Son, specially built His own house, and in whom the only-begotten Son of God, as the reward of your most sincere virginity, confirmed the privilege of His love while hanging on the Cross, saying thus to one of you, "Woman, behold thy son," and then to the other, "Behold thy mother."

In the sweetness therefore of His most sacred love, through which by our Lord's own mouth, as mother and son you were joined to each other, I, a most wretched sinner, commend this day to you my body and soul, that at all hours and moments, inwardly and outwardly, you would be for me steadfast guardians and devout intercessors before God.

Amen.

11

Asking for John's Wisdom and Protection

During the High Middle Ages, the evangelist became the patron saint of consecrated virgins. Large polychrome statues of St. John resting upon Jesus adorned monastery chapels across southern Germany.

The following excerpt, dated to ca. 1200, is taken from a long prayer found in the personal prayerbook of a German nun. She asks the Apostle to take her under his protection, as he did for the Virgin Mary.[76]

I beseech you, pure hero,
You, who were always blessed by God,
St. John the Evangelist,
the blessed Christ indeed entrusted to you
on the Cross His mother, from which time forth,
lord, He did all that you wanted.
God gave you many honors in heaven and on earth,
due to your outstanding merits,
So that you are named apostle and also an evangelist.
Yes, the blessed Christ let you fall asleep on His
breast;
To heaven you were led up,

indeed, you saw there the secrets of the divinity.
God raised you up above all sinful people
when you slumbered on Christ's breast.
From the heights to the depths,
you drank there from wisdom,
most pure lord and pure virgin;
you drank from God's heart there,
from the living fountain, which you saw.
Lord, that eternal life you should give to me,
so that my understanding might inflame itself
with true love so that I may learn the wisdom
that is high, deep, and wide
as she is known to you.
Therefore, lord, take heed
and be my caretaker,
as you, lord, were to the sweet,
pure, and praiseworthy virgin.
Amen.

12

To John, Most Faithful Guardian of Mary

An Augustinian canon regular, Thomas à Kempis (ca. 1380–1471) is the most celebrated author of "Devotio Moderna" spirituality from the Late Middle Ages. Reacting to scholastic theology, this movement emphasized an affective piety centered on the humanity of Christ.

Thomas à Kempis's The Imitation of Christ *is an all-time classic, but a lesser-known collection of his prayers contains a long supplication to Saint John (excerpted here)*[77] *flush with the effusive sentimentality typical of the piety from that period:*

Hail, sweetest Apostle John, most exalted of the evangelists and faithful guardian of Holy Mary, Mother of Jesus.

Overflowing with devotion, I greet you and pay you homage from the depths of my heart, imploring your assistance with loving prayers and sighs.

O most blessed Apostle John! When Jesus was condemned to death by the Cross and covered with wounds, you followed Him, with anguished soul and face sunk with tears, to the place of His crucifixion.

You also accompanied His most sorrowful Mother, the Virgin Mary, together with the compassionate

Magdalene, who, overwhelmed by pain, was on the point of fainting.

The unshakable power of your love for Christ and your heartfelt sharing in His Mother's compassion was shown by the firmness and courage with which you stood by Jesus as He was nailed to the Cross and by His Virgin Mother as she was pierced through with the sword of sorrow.

For that reason, Christ, at His final hour, entrusted His Mother to you in a special way.

O most faithful and chaste guardian of the holy Mother of God, the Virgin Mary!

O You, beloved friend of the Bridegroom of the Church and keeper of the King's most precious treasure!

O most sweet Apostle John, gentle guardian and ever faithful friend, protect me with the weapons of heaven's army and with the standard of the Holy Cross!

Cast from my presence the enemy of Christians, and, when the trying hour of my passing has finally come, obtain my deliverance through the holy name of Jesus!

Amen.

13

Hymn to Saint John, Martyr and Visionary

A patristic-era tradition about a failed attempt to put John to death was later retold in popular lives of the saint. The emperor Domitian (81–96) is said to have ordered John burned alive in boiling oil. When this attempt failed, the apostle was banished to the island of Patmos, where he received the heavenly visions recorded in Revelation.

The following prayer from a Gallican breviary by French poet Jean-Baptise de Santeul (1630–97) addresses John as martyr and visionary.[78]

O pitiless Rome whom rage overtakes,
That Caesar now seek his vengeance to slake,
By sentence decreed against the aged Apostle,
Led off to his death by hands rough and hostile.

Into a sea of fire and hot rumbling oils,
The Martyr is cast, who spurned their idols,
But the flames' reverence and oils' caress,
Let him rise as Victor to triumph and bless.

Banished by Caesar, condemned to exile
He's rapt in the Spirit on a lost desert isle:
To gaze far ahead from lofty abode
And describe hidden sights, those wonders we probe.

O Jesus whose love overcomes earthly might,
Teach us to suffer and share in your plight.
The promised kingdom endures violence still,
So that to seize it, we must follow your will.

To the Father and Son, all glory be rendered
And with the Spirit one in heavenly splendor,
O Blessed Apostle, from whose pen flows a tide,
Whence we draw the faith that makes love abide.

Amen.

14

Oh God! Who Gav'st Thy Servant Grace

This delightful hymn by Reginald Heber (1783–1826), Anglican bishop of Calcutta, asks God to grant us a share in St. John's contemplation while resting on Jesus's breast.[79]

Oh God! who gav'st Thy servant grace,
Amid the storms of life distressed,
To look on thine incarnate face,
And lean on Thy protecting breast:

To see the light that dimly shone,
Eclipsed for us in sorrow pale,
Pure image of the Eternal One!
Through shadows of thy mortal veil!

Grant us, O King of Mercy still,
To feel Thy presence from above,
And in Thy word, and in Thy will,
To hear Thy voice, and know Thy love:

And when the toils of life are done,
And nature waits Thy just decree,
To find our rest beneath Thy throne,
And look, in humble hope, to Thee.

15

Beloved Disciple of Thy Lord

The "Oxford Movement" of the 1830s sought to enrich Anglican piety with older Christian traditions, eventually inspiring converts to Catholicism like St. John Henry Newman. Influenced by this movement, Anglican priest John Chandler published The Hymns of the Primitive Church *in 1837 including this verse translation of an older Latin hymn "Jussu Tyranni pro fide" (below) by French priest Nicolas Letourneux (1640–86).*[80]

Beloved disciple of thy Lord,
Wast thou to exile driven?
Oh never sore thy spirit soared
With fleeter wings to heaven;

He that was dead, and is alive,
Then cheered thine eyes again;
The Lion, strong with death to strive,
The Lamb, for sinners slain.

Oh, then the mysteries were unfurled
Of His triumphant reign,
How martyr blood, through all the world,
His kingdom should maintain.

Then grant us, Lord, with Thee to die,
With Thee again to rise:

With Thee from this vain world to fly,
To meet Thee in the skies.

And now to Him, who vanquished death,
And shows the way to heaven,
To Christ from every human breath,
Be endless praises given. Amen.

Jussu Tyranni pro fide
Pulsus, Johannes, exulas:
Fertur volatu libero
Mens celsa supra sidera.

Illic revelat se tibi
Qui mortuus vivit Deus;
Agnus salutis hostia,
Et morte devicta Leo.

Arcana te vatem docet
Regni sui mysteria,
Pandit cruore martyrum
Ubique spargendam fidem.

Da, Christe, nos tecum mori,
Tecum simul da surgere:
Terrena da contemnere,
Amare da celestia.

Sit laus Patri, laus Filio,
Qui nos, triumphata nece,
Ad astra secum dux vocat,
Compar tibi laus, Spiritus.

16

Saint of the Sacred Heart

Having rested on the Lord's bosom and contemplated His pierced side at the Cross, St. John has long been a theological source for devotion to the Sacred Heart of Jesus. English composer Fr. Frederick Faber (1814–63) captures that tradition in this lovely hymn which appears in the Oratory hymnal of St. Philip Neri and is still sung today.[81]

Saint of the Sacred Heart,
Sweet teacher of the Word;
Partner of Mary's woes
And favorite of thy Lord!
Thou to whom grace was given
To stand where Peter fell,
Whose heart could brook the Cross
Of Him it loved so well!

We know not all thy gifts;
But this Christ bids us see,
That He Who so loved all
Found more to love in thee.
When the last evening came,
Thy head was on His Breast,
Pillowed on earth where now
In heaven the Saints find rest.

Dear Saint I stand far off
With vilest sins oppressed;
Oh may I dare, like thee,
To lean upon His Breast?
His touch could heal the sick,
His voice could raise the dead!
Oh that my soul might be
Where He allows thy head.

The gifts He gave to thee
He gave thee to impart;
And I, too, claim with thee
His Mother and His Heart.
Ah teach me, then, dear Saint!
The secrets Christ taught thee,
The beatings of His Heart,
And how it beat for me. Amen.

17

Word Supreme Before Creation

This well-known hymn by Anglican priest and poet, John Keble (1792–1866), can be sung to the melody of "Tantum Ergo" (8.7.8.7.8.7). It immerses us in St. John's contemplation of the divine mysteries, gliding from the Last Supper, to the Cross, to his heavenly visions while in exile on Patmos.[82]

Word supreme, before creation
Born of God eternally
Who didst will for our salvation
To be born on earth and die;
Well thy saints have kept their station,
Watching till thine hour drew nigh.

Now 'tis come, and faith espies thee:
Like an eagle in the morn,
John in steadfast worship eyes thee,
Thy belov'd, thy latest born:
In Thy glory he descries Thee
Reigning from the tree of scorn.

He, upon Thy Bosom lying,
Thy true tokens learned by heart;
And Thy dearest pledge in dying,
Lord, Thou didst to him impart;
Shew'dst him how, all Grace supplying,
Blood and water from Thee start.

He first hoping and believing
Did beside the grave adore;
Latest he, the warfare leaving,
Landed on the eternal shore;
And his witness we receiving
Own Thee Lord for evermore.

Much he asked in loving wonder,
On Thy bosom leaning, Lord!
In that secret place of thunder,
Answer kind didst Thou accord,
Wisdom for Thy Church to ponder
Till the day of dread award.

Lo! heaven's doors lift up, revealing
How Thy Judgments earthward move;
Scrolls unfolded, trumpets pealing,
Wine cups from the Wrath above:
Yet o'er all a soft voice stealing—
"Little children, trust and love !"

Thee, the Almighty King eternal,
Father of the eternal Word;
Thee, the Father's Word supernal,
Thee, of both, the Breath adored;
Heaven, and earth, and realms infernal
Own, one glorious God and Lord. Amen.

18

O Stream, Lead Us to the Source

French priest and Benedictine abbot, Dom Prosper Guéranger (1805–75) wrote a popular guide to the Catholic liturgical year. The following translates his French prose gloss on a sequence by Adam of St. Victor (pp.85–86) that was used for the vespers of John's legendary martyrdom.[83]

The blessed dwelling place of grace, with their eyes rapt on the High King of glory, sees John filled with God, remade like the Angels, he who described the mysteries of heaven.

Here below, resting on the breast of the Lord, he quenched his thirst at the source of living waters. He was later protected by radiant wonders as he braved the wrath of fire and burning oil.

O martyr! O virgin! O guardian of the Virgin from whom came the glorious Savior, implore for us Him who is the source of all things, He in whom and by whom we live today.

O you, who were cherished more than the others, implore on our behalf Christ who loved you and reconcile us to him.

O stream, lead us to the source!

O hill, guide us up the mountain!

You whom grace made perfect in purity, help us to contemplate the Bridegroom. Amen.

19

O Glorious Apostle

Daily recitation of this prayer was accorded an indulgence by Pope Leo XIII in 1897. That appears to be the earliest reference to this prayer whose precise origin is unknown.[84]

 Glorious Apostle,
who, on account of your virginal purity,
was most beloved by Jesus
as to deserve to lay your head upon His divine breast, and to be left, in His place,
as son to His most holy Mother;
I beg you to inflame within me
a true and ardent love towards Jesus and Mary.

Obtain for me from our Lord that I, too,
with a heart purified from earthly affections,
may be made worthy
to be ever united to Jesus as a faithful disciple,
and to Mary as a devoted son,
both here on earth and eternally in heaven.
Amen.

St. John, the beloved disciple of our Lord, pray for us.

20

Prayer to Saint John for Priests

Although all twelve Apostles shared in Christ's priesthood, St. John has often been revered in Church tradition in the role of a ministerial priest. This prayer, promulgated by St. Pius X (1908), invites clergy to entrust themselves to John as a heavenly intercessor and model of priestly holiness. The following is an excerpt from the Latin original.[85]

We rejoice with you, O blessed John,
who, by virtue of a special predilection,
were called by Christ Jesus
to greater honor than other disciples,
were judged worthy to rest on His heart at Supper and were entrusted by the dying Lord with His own Mother.
We know you have earned this honor
because of your chastity
for, virgin when you were chosen by the Lord,
and virgin you have always remained.
Also, after drinking the living waters of the Gospel from the very Heart of the Lord,

you spoke of the divinity of Christ
with a greater fullness and sublimity.
And because you were inflamed with love,
through contact with the divine Heart,
we are not surprised that,
of all the disciples, you were the only one
to follow Jesus in His Passion,
and thereafter you wrote such pages
that you are rightly called the Apostle of Charity.
It is therefore fitting that we ourselves,
called by divine Goodness to be ministers of Christ
and stewards of the Mysteries of God,
look to you as our model,
just as it is also fitting, we humbly beg you,
that you intercede for us before Jesus and Mary
as our own special patron.
Grant that we may be worthy of our calling,
progress in this vocation, and carry out our
priestly duties with purity of body and soul. Amen.

21

Collect Prayers to Obtain the Gifts of John

A "collect" is a short, formulaic prayer that summarizes the spirit or intention behind an act of communal worship. It is usually composed of a single sentence and thus serves to "gather" (colligere = to draw together) into one petition the prayers of the faithful. It concludes a solemn liturgy or its introductory rites. The following are a few collect prayers for Saint John composed in English.[86]

This collect for December 27th from the Anglican Book of Common Prayer *(1662) is Thomas Cranmer's English translation of an older collect from the Pius V* Roman Missal *(1570), drawing upon John's symbolism of "light":*

Merciful Lord, we beseech thee to cast thy bright beams of light upon thy Church, that it being enlightened by the doctrine of thy blessed Apostle and Evangelist Saint John may so walk in the light of thy truth, that it may at length attain to the light of everlasting life, through Jesus Christ our Lord. Amen.

The English Missal *(1912), a more recent translation of the Pius V* Roman Missal, *uses the above collect for Dec. 27th but the following prayer for the May 6th feast of John's martyrdom:*

O God, who seest us to be sore afflicted by evils on every side: grant, we beseech thee, that the glorious intercession of blessed John, thine Apostle and Evangelist, may be our succour and defence. Through Jesus Christ our Lord . . . Amen.

The most recent English translation of the Paul VI Roman Missal, *third edition (2010) offers an entrance antiphon and collect for Dec. 27th that draw together several threads from the ecclesial tradition. Above all, John is venerated for having transmitted to us the fruits of his contemplation:*

This is John, who reclined on the Lord's breast at supper, the blessed Apostle, to whom celestial secrets were revealed and who spread the words of life through all the world.

O God, who through the blessed Apostle John have unlocked for us the secrets of your Word, grant, we pray, that we may grasp with proper understanding what he has so marvelously brought to our ears. Through our Lord Jesus Christ . . . Amen.

Finally, the Ordinariate's Divine Worship Missal *(2015) retains the May 6 feast and sees in the oil of John's sufferings a blessed anointing that configured him to Christ:*

O God, who with the oil of gladness didst anoint blessed John a companion in the tribulation and patience of the Lord Jesus: grant us likewise to rejoice in the fellowship of Christ's sufferings; that when His glory shall be revealed, we may be glad with exceeding joy. Through the same Christ . . . Amen

22

An Akathist Hymn to Saint John

Akathist hymns are long liturgical prayers sung in solemn assemblies by Byzantine Catholic or Orthodox Christians. The congregation is expected to remain standing for the entire duration of the prayer, hence their name "without sitting" (Ἀκάθιστος). They typically feature thirteen to twenty-four stanzas, each with a poetic prelude followed by a series of invitations to holy joy ("Rejoice . . .").

The following are the first three stanzas from an Akathist him to John used by an Orthodox church in the United States. The entire prayer can be found online.[87]

Stanza 1

Chosen from fisher nets for preaching the Gospel, and from catching fish to catching men into the light of the true knowledge of God, O great Apostle, disciple, friend, and devoted companion of Christ, implore the one true Lover of mankind whom thou didst love with seraphic love to have mercy on us who seek thine intercession with Him and cry to thee:

Rejoice, Apostle John, devoted friend of Christ and Theologian!

When the Sovereign Creator of the angelic hosts and of the whole universe took our flesh and appeared on earth for our salvation, on seeing thee, O blessed John, as He was walking by the Sea of Galilee, He called thee with thy brother to apostolic labor; and thou didst leave thy fisher nets and thy father in the boat, and from then on thou didst follow unswervingly in the Savior's footsteps. Therefore, we cry to thee:

Rejoice, thou who for the love of Christ didst leave thine earthly father!

Rejoice, thou who found in Christ the heavenly Father!

Rejoice, thou who didst despise the world and its delusive pleasures!

Rejoice, thou who didst receive in exchange heavenly blessings!

Rejoice, thou who didst completely subdue thy flesh to thy spirit!

Rejoice, thou who didst subject thy spirit to thy sweetest Lord Jesus!

Rejoice, Apostle John, devoted friend of Christ and Theologian!

Stanza 2

Seeing the spotless purity of thy heart, undarkened by carnal pleasures, Christ the Lord judged thee to be worthy of the vision of mystic revelations, by which thou wast able to fathom the depths of theology and the knowledge of God and couldst preach it for all the world to hear. Therefore, He called thee a son of thunder when thou didst call to Him: Alleluia!

Enlightening thy soul with an understanding of the true knowledge of God, thou didst follow thy good and gracious Master, learning the wisdom that flowed from His lips. On account of thy perfect innocence and virginal chastity, thou was beloved of Christ thy Lord. So, hearken to us who cry to thee thus:

Rejoice, zealot of guilelessness!

Rejoice, guardian of virginity and purity!

Rejoice! teacher of love for God and neighbor!

Rejoice, instructor of good morals!

Rejoice, mirror of humility!

Rejoice, light of Divine Grace!

Rejoice, Apostle John, devoted friend of Christ and Theologian!

Stanza 3

Thou didst clearly realize the power of Christ's divinity hidden under the cloud of weak human nature when He raised to life the daughter of Jairus and then was transfigured on Tabor and chose thee with only two other disciples to be witness of such glorious wonders. Then, knowing that Christ was the True God, from the depths of thy heart thou didst cry to Him: Alleluia!

Having great boldness towards Christ, the Son of God, Who loved thee, thou didst lean upon His breast at the celebration of the Mystical Supper. When the Lord foretold who His betrayer would be, it was only thee who didst have the courage to ask for his name. Therefore, we cry to thee:

Rejoice, beloved disciple of Christ!

Rejoice, true friend of His!

Rejoice, thou who wast chosen by Heaven to lean on the Lord's breast!

Rejoice, thou who didst boldly inquire about the secret of the betrayal!

Rejoice, thou who was nearest to Christ of all of the disciples!

Rejoice, for Christ revealed to thee far more of the divine mysteries than to the other disciples!

Rejoice, Apostle John, devoted friend of Christ and Theologian!

CONTEMPORARY PRAYERS

23

Prayer to John, Our Brother and Friend

The Romanian priest and martyr Blessed Vladimir Ghika (1873–1954) had a strong devotion to St. John and even founded a religious institute inspired by the life and charism of the Evangelist. To his mind, a "beloved disciple" is someone always eager to do what Christ prefers, as Jesus Himself sought to always please the Father (Jn 8:29).[88]

O Saint John,
our elder brother and dear friend,
ever close to us as you are to God,
teach us not only to accomplish what He wills,
but also to anticipate what He prefers,
you, who are the favorite of Him
Whom we should love above all things.
Amen.

24

Entrusting Oneself to Mary like John

Only John's Gospel records the moment when Christ Crucified presents John to Mary as her son and entrusts John to her care as his spiritual mother. Inspired by this testament of the Savior, John has long been associated with Marian piety. On October 8, 2000, St. John Paul II (1920–2005) made this act of entrustment to Mary in the name of the Church, slightly modified here for devotional use.[89]

"Woman, behold your son!" (Jn 19:26)

O Mother, now seated beside our Lord,

the blessed fruit of your womb most pure,

the Word made flesh and the world's Redeemer,

we hear more clearly today the sweet echo of His words entrusting us to you, making you our Mother:

"Woman, behold your son!"

When He entrusted to you the Apostle John,

and with Him the children of the Church and all peoples, Christ did not diminish but affirmed anew the role which is His alone as the Savior of the world.

Therefore, O Mother, like the Apostle John,

we wish to take you into our home (Jn 19:27),

that we may learn from you to become like your Son. "Woman, behold your son!"

Here we stand before you to entrust to your maternal care ourselves, the Church, and the entire world.

Plead for us with your beloved Son

that He may give us in abundance the Holy Spirit,

the Spirit of truth which is the fountain of life.

Receive the Spirit for us and with us,

as happened in the first community gathered around you in Jerusalem on the day of Pentecost.

O Mother, you know the sufferings

and hopes of the Church and the world:

come to the aid of your children in the daily trials

which life brings to each one,

and grant that, thanks to the efforts of all,

the darkness will not prevail over the light.

Amen.

25

Prayer to John for Devotion and Fidelity

This lovely prayer is my English translation of a popular Italian prayer found on devotional cards (santini), websites, and books, "Per quell'angelica purità," whose precise origin is unknown. Among the prayer's special accents are the request for an outlook of faith on life events and the petition for a share in John's heroic perseverance.[90]

By that heavenly purity of heart,
which merited your special privileges
to become the beloved disciple of Jesus Christ,
to rest upon His divine breast,
and to be proclaimed guardian of His holy Mother,
obtain for us, we pray,
O glorious Saint John,
the grace to be inflamed with love for Jesus and Mary.
Teach us to read with devotion the words of your Gospel,
that it may lead us closer to the Lord.
Obtain for us a faith like yours,

that we may see all people, things, and events in the light of the Father's providence.

Ask the Lord to purify our hearts from worldly affections,

that we may remain united to Jesus as faithful disciples

and to Mary as devoted children.

With the same heroic perseverance

that kept you steadfast near the dying Jesus,

watch over us also at the hour of our death,

and obtain for us the grace

to live always with faith

and to carefully imitate your virtues

until that hour when our eternity is decided,

so that we may join you in adoring and praising

the Father, Son, and Holy Spirit,

together with the Blessed Virgin and all the saints.

Amen.

26

A Communal Prayer to Saint John

The early network of Asian churches associated with the Apostle John (cf. Rev 2–3) did not endure in the Church as a distinct institution. Nonetheless, in the modern era, several communities for laity, priests, or religious desire to live out John's charism in today's Church.

The following prayer is used by parishes and religious institutes with a special devotion for Saint John such as the Priests of the Sacred Heart of Jesus (founded by Fr. Leon Dehon in 1878) and the Cenacle Community (founded by Mother Elvira Petrozzi in 1983).[91]

Saint John, young disciple with a pure heart and luminous spirit, when you first met the Lord, you asked, "Master, where do you dwell?" and received the grace to dwell with Him that day.

You then decided to follow and serve Him.

Help us not to miss our opportunities to meet Jesus.

Give us the desire to know Him, the will to seek Him, and the strength to follow Him.

Grant us to know, even in hard times, how to rest our hearts on the Heart of Christ, as you did at the Last Supper.

You who, more than any other, knew the depths of God's love and recognized yourself as Jesus' "beloved disciple,"

Help us to contemplate the living presence of Christ, so that, like you, we may recognize ourselves as His "beloved children."

Your life of purity, in imitation of the Lord, inspires us to desire pure thoughts, words, and deeds.

John, you who welcomed Mary into your home as Mother, let her presence never abandon us, and may her intercession preserve and increase our faith.

Help us to run with perseverance to the destinations that Providence indicates, so that we may, like you, announce to others the joy of Christ's resurrection.

Saint John, apostle and evangelist, pray for us!

27

Prayer to Saint John for Parents

In the biblical Epistles of John, the author addresses the faithful with the tenderness and concern of a loving father. That spiritual fatherhood is reflected in this popular prayer for parents and families.[92]

St. John, chaste and favored disciple of our Lord, with the loving heart of a father, you watched over the faithful entrusted to your care:

"And now, dear children, abide in Him."

O blessed son of our dear Lady, how greatly I desire that my children and I may resemble you in purity of heart, in love for Christ, and in devotion towards His Virgin Mother!

Watch over us from heaven and implore Divine Mercy to fill our hearts with the same graces you enjoyed.

Pray for us, that we may love one another and remain united in God's love.

We confidently ask for these blessings through your intercession, O beloved disciple of Jesus and devoted son of Mary. Amen.

28

Litany to Saint John (I)[93]

Kyrie eleison,
Kyrie eleison,

Christe eleison,
Christe eleison

Kyrie eleison,
Kyrie eleison.

Christ hear us,
Christ hear us.

God, our Heavenly Father,
have mercy on us.

Son, Redeemer of the world,
have mercy on us.

Holy Spirit of God,
have mercy on us.

Holy Trinity, One God,
have mercy on us.

Holy Mary, Queen of Apostles.
pray for us.

Saint John, son of Zebedee,
pray for us. (repeat for the following petitions)

Saint John, son of Thunder,

Saint John, fisherman of Galilee,

Saint John, brother of James,

Saint John, disciple of John the Baptist,

Saint John, called by Christ to the Company of the Twelve,

Saint John, beloved disciple of the Lord Jesus,

Saint John, faithful hearer of the Good News,

Saint John, wonderful Apostle,

Saint John, witness to the resurrection of Jairus's daughter,

Saint John, who contemplated the Lord's glory on Mount Tabor,

Saint John, who rested on Christ's chest at the Last Supper,

Saint John, who received the precious Body and Blood from the Hands of Christ,

Saint John, chosen to keep vigil in Gethsemane,

Saint John, who stood with Mary at the foot of the Cross,

Saint John, who heard the last words of the Lord,

Saint John, protector of the Mother of Christ,

Saint John, who ran to the Tomb on Easter morning,

Saint John, who prayed in the Cenacle before Pentecost,

Saint John, inspired author of the Gospel,

Saint John, writer of the Epistles and the Apocalypse,

Saint John, servant of the Savior,

Saint John, our advocate before the throne of God,

Saint John, model of holy life,

Lamb of God, who takes away the sins of the world,
spare us, Lord.

Lamb of God, who takes away the sins of the world,
hear us, Lord.

Lamb of God, who takes away the sins of the world,
have mercy on us.

Pray for us, Saint John the Apostle,
that we may become worthy of the promises of Christ.

Let us pray:

God, our Father, who gave humankind Your Only Son, in His Name and through the intercession of Saint John the Apostle, we humbly ask you to listen to the prayers of the Church of Christ and of people everywhere who earnestly seek to do Your holy will.

Amen.

29

Litany to Saint John (II)[94]

Lord have mercy.
Lord have mercy.

Christ have mercy.
Christ have mercy.

Lord have mercy.
Lord have mercy.

Christ hear us.
Christ graciously hear us.

God, the Father of Heaven,
have mercy on us.

God, the Son, Redeemer of the world,
have mercy on us.

God, the Holy Spirit,
have mercy on us.

Holy Trinity, One God,
have mercy on us.

Saint John the Theologian,
pray for us. (repeat for the following petitions)

Apostle of Christ,

Evangelist who bore witness to the Word of God,

Evangelist who recorded the testimony of Jesus,

Evangelist of the Word made Flesh,

Beloved Disciple who rested on the Heart of the Lord,

Witness of the Transfiguration,

Defender of Virgins,

Model of chastity,

Teacher of charity,

Disciple who touched the Word of Life,

Evangelist of the Heart of Christ,

Son of Zebedee the fisherman,

Son of Salome the myrrh-bearer,

Brother of Saint James,

Son of Thunder,

Follower of the Baptist,

Disciple who bore witness,

Disciple who drank of the heavenly streams,

Disciple present at the foot of the Cross,

Beloved Disciple to whom was entrusted the Virgin Mother,

Spiritual son of Mary,

Disciple who ran to the tomb,

Herald of the Resurrection,

Disciple who cried out "It is the Lord!"
Rampart against Heresy,
Defender of the Lord's Divinity,
Priest of the Holy Eucharist,
Companion of Peter,
Pillar of the Church,
Witness cast into a cauldron of boiling oil,
Exile of Patmos,
Prophet of the New Creation,
Bishop and herald at Knock,
Our Brother in Christ,
Companion in tribulation,
Companion in the Kingdom,
Companion in patience,
Lover of Sunday,
Presbyter to the elect,
Prophet to the seven churches,
Defender of the aged,
Mirror of chastity,
Teacher of heavenly charity,
Mystical visionary,
Seer of the heavenly Jerusalem,

Lamb of God who takes away the sins of the world,
spare us, O Lord.

Lamb of God who takes away the sins of the world,
graciously hear us, O Lord.

Lamb of God who takes away the sins of the world,
have mercy on us.

Let us pray:

Almighty and Eternal God,
in Your goodness, enlighten Your Church,
we pray, by the light of the teaching
of Saint John the Evangelist, Your Apostle,
so that she may come into possession
of the everlasting treasures You promise.
We ask this through our Lord Jesus Christ
Your Son who lives and reigns with You
in the unity of the Holy Spirit,
God forever and ever.

Amen.

30

Novena to Saint John[95]

Day 1

Jesus, You revealed Yourself as the "gate" through whom we must pass to find eternal life. Help us follow in the footsteps of Your Apostle John and respond to Your call with a sincere faith.

Saint John, Fisher of Men, at the very sound of our Lord's voice, you put down your net and followed Jesus. You embraced God's will for your life, stepping out with radical trust. Walk alongside me in my journey with Christ.

Teach me to open my heart to God as you did, so that I may recognize His presence in my daily tasks. Help me know the sound of Jesus's voice and embrace His call.

Pray that I may courageously step out of my boat, willing to leave everything else behind, and become a faithful and humble disciple of Christ.

Pray also for the intention which I hold in my heart today . . .

Saint John the Apostle, pray for us! Amen.

Day 2

Jesus, Word of God, You existed since the beginning and brought everything into creation. Yet

You willingly made Your dwelling among us. Help us to truly encounter You like Your Apostle John.

Saint John, for three years you witnessed the incredible power of Christ by living alongside Him. You saw the sick healed, the lame walk, and the dead raised. You saw Christ turn water into wine and feed thousands with only a bit of fish and bread.

To you, Jesus revealed Himself as the fulfillment of God's promise. Help increase my faith.

Open to me the presence of God in Scripture and in my daily life. Instill in me a deep love for the Word of God. Show me how to make my heart a suitable dwelling place for Him.

Pray that I may always recognize the gifts Jesus desires to give me and that I may always praise Him. Please, offer sincerest gratitude on my behalf to our Heavenly Father.

Pray also for the intention which I entrust to you today . . .

Saint John the Apostle, pray for us! Amen.

Day 3

Jesus, Light of the World, You promised Your followers the light of life. Reveal to me Your glory through Your Apostle John.

Beloved John, Apostle and friend of Jesus, you were permitted to witness the radiance of God's splendor during the Transfiguration of our Lord. Help lead me out of the darkness of my sin and shame into the presence of God.

Alongside Peter and your brother James, Christ revealed His divinity to you, and you heard the voice of the Father affirm it. Show me how to live as a close friend of Jesus, that I may know Him as you did. Help me live as a child of the Light, eager to follow His commandments.

Pray that the light of Christ illuminate my mind and heart that I may one day share in His glory.

Please pray also for the special intention which I bring to you today . . .

Saint John the Apostle, pray for us! Amen

Day 4

Jesus, Bread of Life, You promised those who would come to You that they would never hunger or thirst. Instill in us the same Eucharistic devotion of Saint John.

O beloved Apostle of Christ, you heard the Divine Heart beating as you rested your head on the breast of our Lord. To you, the mysteries of heaven have been revealed. Bring me ever closer to the heart of Christ.

Your feet were washed by your Teacher and Lord before He nourished your soul with His very self. He gave you the commandment to "take and eat," inviting you to partake in His eternal life.

Help me recognize the True Presence of Jesus in the Eucharist and kindle in me a blazing love for the Most Blessed Sacrament. Increase my desire to unite myself to Christ, especially at the celebration of Holy Mass.

Please pray also for the intention closest to my heart . . .

Saint John the Apostle, pray for us! Amen.

Day 5

Jesus, True Vine, You asked that we remain always with You, for we cannot bear fruit by our own merit. Through the intercession of Saint John the Apostle, give us the grace to abide in Your love.

Saint John, you went with Jesus and the two other Apostles to the Mount of Olives to pray with our Lord as He agonized over His impending Passion.

Three times during this first holy hour, Christ was saddened to find you asleep. The spirit was willing, but the flesh was weak. Be with me during my own trials.

Help me embrace my suffering and to run wholeheartedly to the Lord, especially in times of weakness and distress. Keep me close to Christ.

Pray for me so that I may be found ready and alert when my time has come. Pray also for the leaders of our Church, that they might always stand vigilant, ready to protect their flock from all that could harm them.

Finally, please pray for the special intention I bring to you today . . .

Saint John the Apostle, pray for us! Amen.

Day 6

Jesus, Good Shepherd, You humbly laid down Your life for us, Your sheep. Help us learn from Saint John the Apostle how to offer ourselves in return to You.

Saint John, Apostle of Charity, you stood at the foot of the Cross, the only one of the Twelve to remain at Jesus's side during His darkest hour, bringing comfort to our suffering Savior.

You stood close enough for the Precious Blood of Our Lord to fall upon you as it poured from His hands and feet, one of the first receivers of this priceless gift. Bring me close enough to kiss the wounds of my Savior.

Help me to drink deeply of the streams of mercy and love that flowed from the pierced side of Christ.

Show me how to cling to Jesus especially in times of great difficulty and help me to console His Sacred Heart by uniting my sufferings to His. Pray that I may always abide in His love.

Please bring my petition to the foot of Christ's Cross . . .

Saint John the Apostle, pray for us! Amen.

Day 7

Jesus, You are the Resurrection and the Life. You promised that those who followed You would never die. Like your Apostle John, bring us into Your eternal life.

Blessed John, the disciple whom Jesus loved, at the news of Christ's Resurrection, you hastened to the empty tomb.

With your own eyes, you witnessed His triumph over sin and death. Help me enter into the joy and promise of the Resurrection.

Teach me to pursue Christ, even when it seems like all is lost. Show me how to trust in God's infinite goodness and power in spite of my sin and failing. Encourage me to always run toward the Savior.

Pray that all souls, especially those closest to me, may come to Christ. Pray also for me to remain steadfast in the hope that I may dwell with God for eternity.

Please pray for the intention which I bring to you today . . .

Saint John the Apostle, pray for us! Amen.

Day 8

Jesus, Word made flesh, the Father's love became incarnate through Your Immaculate Mother. Help us, like John, to live as one of her children.

O Beloved Disciple, from the Cross our Lord entrusted you to the care of His Blessed Mother, and her to you.

From that moment on, you took Mary into your home. You protected and cared for her until she reached the end of her earthly life. Teach me to love and honor the Mother of God as you did.

Help increase my devotion to our Blessed Mother. Help me draw closer to her so that she may bring me closer to her Son. Pray that she be with me at the moment of my death to lead me into heaven.

Please pray also through the intercession of the Blessed Mother for the special intention I bring to you today . . .

Saint John the Apostle, pray for us! Amen.

Day 9

Jesus, you are the Way, the Truth, and the Life. Through you alone can we come to our Heavenly Father. Inspire us to live like your Apostle John and proclaim the Truth with missionary zeal.

Saint John, Missionary Disciple of Christ, your love for Jesus inspired your every word and deed. Your life became a profound witness to the glory of God. Help me embrace Christ's call to go and make disciples.

Before Christ, you lived as a humble fisherman, yet your words and example brought countless souls to Him, your testimony still reaching through time. You speak to us to this day through your Gospel, continuing to share the goodness of God with His Church.

Show me how to open my mind and heart to the Holy Spirit and teach me to follow His inspirations. Grant me courage that I can be bold, as you were, in proclaiming the Good News to everyone I meet.

Please pray for the special intention I bring to you today . . .

Saint John the Apostle, pray for us! Amen.

ENDNOTES

1 By my count, the *Catechism of the Catholic Church*, 2nd edition (2000), cites the Johannine writings 114 times in "Part Four: Christian Prayer" §2558–2865. 106 different passages or verses are cited.

2 See Fiore, "Johannine Identity and Its Consequences for Spirituality" in *Spirituality in John's Gospel* (Eugene, OR: Pickwick, 2023), 215–80.

3 Francis J. Moloney, *The Gospel of John*, ed. Daniel J. Harrington (Collegeville, MN: Liturgical Press, 1998), 34.

4 Rudolf Bultmann, *The Gospel of John*, trans. George R. Beasley-Murray. (Oxford: Basil Blackwell, 1971), 14.

5 Robert Karris, *Prayer and the New Testament: Jesus and His Communities at Worship* (New York: Crossroad, 2000), 85, 87–88.

6 "And we have seen his glory" (Jn 1:14 NRSV).

7 "And from his fulness we have all received, grace upon grace" (Jn 1:16 RSVCE).

8 St. John Chrysostom, *Homilies on the Gospel of John* 14.1, NPNF 1 14:47).

9 "The light shines in the darkness, and the darkness did not overcome it" (Jn 1:5 NRSV).

10 St. John Paul II, *Redemptoris Mater*, §21.

11 "Lord, give me this water" (Jn 4:15 CPDV).

12 Origen of Alexandria on Jacob's well, *Commentary on the Gospel of John,* 13:6–7, 26–31, trans. Ronald E. Heine (Washington, D.C.: The Catholic University of America Press, 1993), 70, 74–75.

13 St. Teresa of Avila, *Book of Her Life* 30.19; *Soliloquy* no.9.

14 "Lord, come down before my child dies" (Jn 4:49 LSV).

15 "Lord, give us this bread always" (Jn 6:34 RSVCE).

16 Pope Benedict XVI, *Jesus of Nazareth: From the Baptism in the Jordan to the Transfiguration,* trans. Adrian J. Walker (London: Bloomsbury, 2008), 267.

17 "Lord, he whom you love is ill" (Jn 11:3 NRSV).

18 "We want to see Jesus" (Jn 12:21 CPDV).

19 St. John Paul II, "Message for World Youth Day," February 22, 2004.

20 St. Teresa of Avila, *Way of Perfection* 25.1.

21 St. Gregory of Nyssa, *In Canticum Canticorum,* Homily 2, 801D as cited by Blaise Arminjon, *The Cantata of Love*, trans. Nelly Marans (San Francisco: Ignatius Press, 1988), 252.

22 St. Gregory the Great, *Moralia in Job*, bk. V, ch. 6.

23 St. John Paul II, *Pastores Dabo Vobis*, no.46.

24 St. Thomas Aquinas, *Commentary on the Gospel of John*, no.294.

25 For this interpretation of Nathanael under the tree, Schnackenburg cites a rabbinical dictum and the custom of doctors of the law. Rudolf Schnackenburg, *The Gospel According to John*, vol.1, trans. Kevin Smyth (London: Burns & Oates, 1968), 317.

26 "Now we know that he is indeed the Savior of the world" (Jn 4:42 NLT).

27 St. Thomas Aquinas, *Commentary on the Gospel of John*, no.626–28.

28 "Lord, to whom shall we go? You have the words of eternal life" (Jn 6:68 RSVCE).

29 See Vatican II, *Lumen Gentium*, §25 or *Code of Canon Law* §752.

30 See *Catechism of the Catholic Church*, 2nd ed. §1783–85.

31 See *Dignitatis Humanae* §14 or Congregation for the Doctrine of the Faith, *Donum Veritatis* §28.

32 This insight and the later remark about Martha's understanding of eschatology draw from Cornelis Bennema, *Encountering Jesus: Character Studies in the Gospel of John*, 2nd ed. (Minneapolis: Fortress Press, 2014), 259–266.

33 See Sandra Schneiders, "Death in the Community of Eternal Life" 53n26, as cited by Bennema, 262n11.

34 See St. Thomas Aquinas, *Summa Theologiae*, IIa IIae q.188 a.6 and IIIa q.40 a.1.

35 See Aquinas, *Commentary on the Gospel of John*, §1806; §2487; and §2592.

36 Regarding the probable seating position at the Last Supper in John 13 and its significance, see note 45 below.

37 See Thomas Aquinas, *Summa Theologiae*, IIa IIae q.83 a.12; on sacred gestures like sacrifice, q.85 a.1; expressing interior offering of the soul q.85 a.2.

38 Romano Guardini, *Sacred Signs*, trans. Grace Branham (St. Louis, MO: Pio Decimo Press, 1956), 18.

39 "And they remained with him that day" (Jn 1:39 NRSV).

40 First line from a prayer by St. Elizabeth of the Trinity, as cited by *The Catechism of the Catholic Church*, 2nd ed., §260 (Vatican City: Libreria Editrice Vaticana, 2000). "As the beloved in the lover" (*sicut amatum in amante*) from St. Thomas Aquinas, *Summa Theologiae*, Ia q.43 a.3.

41 "And the house was filled with the fragrance of the perfume" (Jn 12:3 NASB).

42 For historical details related in this paragraph, see Craig S. Keener, *The Gospel of John: A Commentary* (Grand Rapids, MI: Baker Academic, 2012), 862–64.

43 First words from St. Ignatius of Loyola's famous *Suscipe* prayer from the *Spiritual Exercises* §234. See his *Spiritual Exercises and Selected Works*,

ed. George E. Ganss (Mahwah: Paulist Press, 1991), 177.

44 "There was reclining on Jesus' bosom one of His disciples, whom Jesus loved" (Jn 13:23 NASB).

45 The description of the probable seating arrangement and its significance are drawn from Keener, *The Gospel of John*, 915–16.

46 Origen of Alexandria, *Commentary on the Gospel of John*, book 1, 1:23 and book 2, 32:264.

47 Ephrem the Syrian, *Hymns on Virginity*, 25:2–4; Jerome of Stridon, *Commentary on Matthew*, Preface, pp. 2.

48 Saint Thomas Aquinas, *Commentary on the Gospel of John*, no.1807.

49 St. John Paul II, *Ecclesia de Eucharistia*, no. 25.

50 For the tradition of depicting the Virgin Mary's "swoon" at the Cross and Counter-Reformation corrections, see *The Sixteenth Century Italian Paintings, volume 1: Brescia, Bergamo and Cremona*, ed. Nicolas Penny (New Haven: Yale University Press, 2004), 26–28.

51 "So they put a sponge full of the wine on a branch of hyssop and held it to his mouth" (Jn 19:29 NRSV).

52 Mother Teresa, *Where There Is Love, There Is God*, ed. Brian Kolodiejchuk. (New York: Doubleday, 2010), 192.

53 St. Therese of Lisieux, *Story of a Soul*. 3rd edition, trans. John Clarke (Washington, D.C.: ICS, 1997), A45v–46v.

54 Although sometimes translated as "common wine" (NAB), the drink offered to Jesus crucified was most likely *poska*, a mixture of wine-vinegar diluted with water that was a common drink for workers and soldiers. See Keener, *The Gospel of John*, 1147. For Jesus's thirst having spiritual value, see Karris, *Prayer and the New Testament*, 109–110.

55 From *Donatien Mollat, Saint Jean: maître spirituel* (Paris: Beauchesne, 1976), 143, 141. My translation.

56 For the customary Jewish table blessing likely used by Jesus, see Keener, *The Gospel of John*, 667.

57 On Jesus's unspoken life of prayer with the Father, see Andrew T. Lincoln, "God's Name, Jesus' Name, and Prayer in the Fourth Gospel," in *Into God's Presence: Prayer in the New Testament*, ed. Richard Longenecker (Grand Rapids, MI: Eerdmans, 2001), 159–60.

58 On the significance of the (Gentile) "Greeks" coming to see Jesus, see Raymond E. Brown, *The Gospel according to John I–XII*, 466n20 (Garden City: Doubleday, 1966), 469–70.

59 "Father, the hour has arrived: glorify your Son . . . so that he may give eternal life to all those whom you have given to him" (Jn 17:1–2 CPDV).

60 In the prayer of John 17, Jesus "bares his heart" according to Lincoln, "God's Name" (cited in note 57), 171.

61 Cyprian of Carthage, "On the Unity of the Church" §7. In *Ante-Nicene Fathers*, vol.5, trans. Ernest Walls (Peabody: Hendrickson, 1994), 423.

62 On John's realized eschatology and beholding Jesus's glory in the present, see Keener, 1063–64, and Fiore, *Spirituality in John's Gospel*, esp. "seeing God" 324–25, 327 and "contemplation" 331–32.

63 St. Thomas Aquinas, *Commentary on John*, 19.5.2447.

64 See the commentary on Jesus's thirst by various saints collected in Joseph Langford, *Mother Teresa's Secret Fire*. (Huntington, VA: Our Sunday Visitor, 2008), 287–96. "Are we truly seeking . . ." Mother Teresa, "Letter to the MC Sisters" March 6, 1992—both as cited by Langford, 288 and 281.

65 On Jn 19:28 as a prayer addressed to God, see Karris, *Prayer and the New Testament*, 108–111.

66 Author unknown. English version borrowed (amended) from the Greek Orthodox Archdiocese of America: https://www.goarch.org/-/feast-of-the-holy-and-glorious-apostle-and-evangelist-john-the-theologian. L.6 amended from "the persistent cloud of nations."

67 Excerpt from "Hymn to Virginity XV" (amended) in *Ephrem the Syrian, Hymns*, trans. Kathleen McVey (Mahwah, NJ: PaulistPress, 1989), 326–27. Str.4 l.1 "too" removed; l.3 you, chaste disciple, for "the chaste youth"; l.5 Virginity for "O Virginity He"; 1.6 onlookers for "the Watchers"; ll.6–7 skipped; Str.5 l.7 silent for "mute"; satisfy for "restrain"; l.8 a for "is"; l.9 an enigma for seekers for "vexation for the inquirers".

68 Only strophes 1–6 (of nine) appear here. Latin text with English translation (amended) from Abbot Prosper Guéranger, *The Liturgical Year: Christmas, book 1*, trans. Laurence Shepherd (Fitzwilliam, NH: Loreto Publications, 2000), 265–66. Str.1 honored by the love of Christ for "the honoured loved one of Jesus"; str. 3 catches for "takes"; life of men for "light of the world" str.4 swam for "swain".

69 My translation from the Latin found in Andrea Cavallini, *La penna del pavone: Bibbia ed esegesi in Giovanni Scoto Eriugena* (Rome: Città Nuova, 2016), 65n4.

70 My translation (shortened) from the French found in Jean Villepelet, *Les plus beaux textes sur St Jean l'évangéliste* (Paris: La Colombe, 1953), 78. Omitted verses 3, 8–11.

71 My translation from the Latin found in Petri Damiani, *Carmina et Preces*, ed. M. Lokrantz and U. Facchini (Rome: Città Nuova, 2007),

228–29. I finished the doxology which the editors left abbreviated.

72 Excerpt from Anselm's 1st prayer to John (vv.1–24, 103–111) from *The Prayers and Meditations of St. Anselm with the Proslogion*, ed. Benedicta Ward (New York: Penguin, 1973), 157–62. Amended: ll. 3–4 and most beloved apostle for "best beloved of the apostles"; of the Lord for "of God"; l. 13 poor for "little" and stands guilty before for "is accused of God"; l.15 be spared from God's just punishment for "turn from himself the threat of the wrath of God"; l.20 with God whose retribution he fears for "with him whom he fears as an avenger"; l.24 you obtain from God whatever you ask for "you can do what you wish before God." L.103 by virtue of that same privilege for "by that very thing."

73 English version (excerpted) from *On Love*, ed. Hugh Feiss (Turnhout: Brepols, 2011), 237–39. Amended: v.3 Him for "him"; v.4 His for "his"; This virgin, John, for "this virgin"; her for "the one" (for clarity); vv.6–13 omitted; v.14 the divine added to "the beginning; v.15 omitted.

74 My translation of antiphon no.26 (in full) and response no.27 (excerpted) from the Latin found in *Louanges*, trans. Laurence Moulinier (Paris: La différence, 1990), 50–52.

75 English version (excerpted) from https://www.preces-latinae.org/thesaurus/BVM/OIntemerata.html.

76 English version (excerpted) from Jeffrey Hamburger, *St. John the Divine* (Berkley: University of California Press, 2002), 167–69. Omitted ll.11, 16–17, 27–34. Amended l. 10 due to your outstanding merits for "with much great worthiness"; l.42 take heed for "be instructed".

77 My selection and translation from the longer Latin prayer "Oratio de privilegiis praecipua amoris beati Iohannis Evangelistae" in *Opera Omnia*, vol.3, ed. Michael J. Pohl (St. Louis, MO: Herder, 1904), 373–78. Shown here 373 ll.16–22 and 375, l.4 to 376, l.2.

78 My selection and verse translation from the French given by Jean Villepelet *Les Plus Beaux Textes sur St Jean l'Evangeliste* (Paris: La Colombe, 1953), 109–110. Shown are str. 7–11.

79 Version (amended) from *Hymns Written and Adapted to the Weekly Service of the Church Year* (Murray, 1827), 26, as cited by http://www.hymntime.com/tch/htm/o/g/w/g/ogwgavst.htm. Str.3 Grant us for "Be ours"; str.4 just for "dread" decree; humble for "certain" hope.

80 English verse translation from *The Hymns of the Primitive Church*, ed. John Chandler (London: Parker, 1837), 51–52. Contractions removed.

81 *The St. Gregory Hymnal and Catholic Choir Book*, ed. Nicola A. Montani (Philadelphia, PA: St. Gregory Guild, 1920), 160–61. Contractions removed.

82 From *Hymns Ancient and Modern for Use in the Services of the Church*, ed. William Henry Monk

(London: Clowes & Sons, 1861) as cited by "Saint Augustine's Lyre" blog: https://tosingistopraytwice.wordpress.com/2017/11/19/word-supreme-before creation/.

83 My translation from the French prose gloss on the sequence by Prosper Guéranger, *L'année liturgique: Le temps pascal, tome II* (Paris, Alfred Mame et Fils, 1926), 526–27. Omitted third stanza.

84 Author unknown. English version found on https://saintmichaelusa.org/1227-st-john-evangelist/.

85 My translation from the Latin in *Enchiridion Indulgentiaum*, revised edition (Typis Polyglottis Vaticanis, 1952), 568–69.

86 *The Book of Common Prayer*, 1662 edition with additions & deviations (London: Eyre and Spottiswoode, 1927), 120; *The English Missal* (Norwich: Canterbury Press, 2001), 649. *Daily Roman Missal according to the Roman Missal*, Third Edition (Downers' Grove, IL: Midwest Theological Forum, 2010), 2028; *Divine Worship Missal* (London: Catholic Truth Society, 2015), 728.

87 Author unknown. Version (abridged) from "Saint John the Evangelist Orthodox Church in Pheonix, Arizona" https://www.stjohnaz.org/about-us/our-patron-saint/.

88 My translation from the French found on https://www.vladimirghika.ro/textes-des-prieres-composees-par-mgr-ghika-a-lusage-de-la-famille-de-saint-jean-a-auberive/.

89 English version found on https://www.vatican.va/content/johnpaulii/en/homilies/2000/documents/hf_jpii_hom_20001008_act-entrustment-mary.html. Amendments for devotional use: §1, omitted reference to Jubilee Year; added now seated before our Lord; omitted "You are the splendor . . ."; §2–3 omitted; §4 "May the Spirit . . ." omitted; §5 "To you, Dawn . . ." omitted.

90 Author unknown. My translation of "Preghiera a san Giovanni Evangelista" in Antonio Piñero, Vita dei Santi: *San Giovanni Evangelista*, trans. Sonia Ascoli (Milano: RBA Italia, 2015), 69.

91 Author unknown. My translation from the Italian found on https://www.comunitacenacolo.it/official/index.php? option=com_content&view=article&layout=edit&id=354.

92 My own revised version of a longer prayer found on https://catholicharboroffaithandmorals.com/St.%20John% 20 Popup.html.

93 Author unknown. Version (amended) from "God Who is Rich in Mercy" blog: https://www.facebook.com/photo. php?fbid=659769549702503&id=100070083907593&set=a.382904227389038&locale=pl_PL.

94 Author unknown. Version (amended) from "The Word is Quiet Here" blog: https://www.thomryng.com/amateurmonk/prayers-and-meditations/litany-of-saint-john/.

95 Author unknown. Version from "Pray More Novenas" website: https://www.praymorenovenas.com/st-john-the-apostle.

Image Credits

Cover image: Symbols of Four Evangelists © Luna Solvot - Cliparto.

Page ii: *Saint John* by Jaques Stella, wooduct. National Gallery of Art / Rosenwald Collection. In the public domain via Wikimedia Commons.

Page xxii: *St. John the Evangelist* by William Faithorne, (1616–91), engraving (1657), Private Collection. Photo © Tom Graves Archive / Bridgeman Images.

Page 72: *Saint John* by Hans Baldung Grien, woodcut, 1519. National Gallery of Art / Rosenwald Collection. In the public domain via Wikimedia Commons.